ARCHITECTURE ON DISPLAY

Architecture on Display:
On the History of the Venice Biennale of Architecture

ARCHITECTURAL ASSOCIATION LONDON

Contents

Preface

Brett Steele

The Venice Biennale of Architecture is an integral part of contemporary architectural culture. And not only for its arrival, like clockwork, every 730 days (every other August) as the rolling index of curatorial (much more than material, social or spatial) instincts within the world of architecture. The biennale's importance today lies in its vital dual presence as both register and infrastructure, recording the impulses that guide not only architecture but also the increasingly international audiences created by (and so often today, nearly subservient to) contemporary architectures of display. As the title of this elegant book suggests, 'architecture on display' is indeed the larger cultural condition serving as context for the popular success and 30-year evolution of this remarkable event.

To look past its most prosaic features as an architectural gathering measured by crowd size and exhibitor prowess, the biennale has become something much more than merely a regularly scheduled (if at times unpredictably organised) survey of architectural experimentation: it is now the key global embodiment of the curatorial bias of not only contemporary culture but also architectural life, or at least of how we imagine, represent and display that life.

The history of successive biennales isn't just its register, as if a windsock, of architectural fashion, taste or interest. By this stage, the biennale has itself become a kind of living record – of architecture's own contemporary struggle as a form of cultural production on the one hand, and that production on (and not only *of*) display on the other. Seeing these dual tendencies as commensurate and equal, or as simply parallel and opposed, is simply too crude a (dialectical) view of knowledge (let alone architectural knowledge) today.

We should recall, for example, just how many of modern architecture's key battles were fought long before the Venice architecture biennale, on sites such as world expositions (remember Mies in Barcelona), international exhibitions (including the 'International Style' proclaimed by a New York museum nearly a century ago), or landmark cultural events (the architecturally staged 'Kitchen Debate' between Nixon and Khrushchev in 1959, as one example among many). In effect, all of these demonstrate something of the extended legacy of displaying and exhibiting architectural culture, well before Venice's more recent and decidedly contemporary twist in the form we now know as the architectural bienniale.

What the proven template of the biennale offers above all, then, is perhaps this: the possibility that, by putting the work and thinking of architecture's key protagonists and prodigies on display every two years in the Arsenale and Giardini, architecture might yet still exist *as* (and not only *through*) its own forms of communication. In the case of Venice, this amounts to the forms of display promoting architectural agendas and interests, and not only projects or personalities. The display of architectural ambitions, obsessions even; and perhaps even of architectural ideas – this is certainly something confirmed in the statements and remarks captured so vividly in the following book, marvellously edited and organised by Aaron Levy and William Menking in dialogue with the key curators whose ingenuity, energy and ambition defined – and largely designed – the biennale we know today.

Given that the art biennale in Venice is now well over a century old and film enthusiasts have been going to their annual festival in Venice almost since the medium's invention (Frank Capra's *It Happened One Night* was featured at the inaugural festival there in 1932), architecture's relatively late arrival in 1980 is only the first of many larger questions about architectural culture today that this collection begins to explore. The largely oral format, as a series of recorded conversations with some of the immensely talented shapers of successive biennials and of larger architectural discussion, is one of the book's great accomplishments. Oral history is returned to an event itself dependent upon the idea of exchange, discussion and communication (all traits at odds with a discipline like architecture, and its too frequently witnessed belief in one-way communication, singular forms of representation or signature styles, monologues and declarations). The contribution provided by this book, as a genuine extension of the biennial itself, is an immense – provisional, preliminary but genuinely valuable – aid. My thanks here to Aaron Levy and William Menking for bringing this project to us at the AA School in London; to all the curators for their participation in the conversations themselves; and to the wonderful editors and designers at AA Publications who so swiftly and assuredly (over a matter of a few short weeks) created and then delivered the book to Venice in time for its biennale launch.

Brett Steele
Director, AA School of Architecture

Introduction

Aaron Levy

Although the Venice Biennale for architecture is
considered to be one of the most prestigious forums
for architecture in the world, its history remains
relatively unknown and is marked by fundamental
tensions. These include its very point of origin,
as well as its integration with economic tourism
and nation-state representation, its relationship to
the art biennale, and its dependence on theatrical
models of display. With these tensions in mind,
William Menking and I began to conduct a living
history of the architecture biennale in December
2009. Through conversations with past directors
of the biennale, we sought to understand the
cultural, political and economic conflicts that
have shaped each biennale, and the way in which
the biennale is itself a living institution evolving
in time. We were particularly interested in how
the architecture biennale has developed from a
relatively modest and informal proposition in the
1970s and 80s – one that intermittently explored
the social function of architecture and questions
of audience and display – to its present stature as
one of the foremost architectural exhibitions.

　　　If there is an urgency to this project, it is
not only on account of the late Aldo Rossi, director
of the 1985 and 1986 biennales, whose work was

itself cognisant of the importance of historical memory, and whose voice is sadly missing from these pages. The Venice architecture biennale itself constitutes a forgotten history whose recovery has consequences for contemporary practice. Since its first articulation in 1895, the biennale has, in spite of its international visibility and attendance, remained one of the least accessible sites for archival research. As the pulse of the present subsides after each year's biennale is over, the intensity of the experimental dispositions presented in Venice recedes into memory. It is thus important to unpack the implications of the traces that remain in archives and the public sphere more generally. In speaking with each of the past directors of the Venice architecture biennale (henceforth referred to simply as the biennale), we therefore hope to supplement the official record with a more anecdotal and informal telling, one that acknowledges the individual passions that mark their respective exhibitions. The traces they provide also help us recover the forgotten history of cultural experimentation that has taken place at each biennale, and the social conditions that provide a context for these experiments.

Readers may notice that there is not one particular question or finding that emerges from these conversations. Instead, we have approached this project throughout with a sensibility of curiosity and openness towards the individual recollections and experiences. Moreover, these conversations do not seek to recapitulate the exhibitions themselves but rather explore the questions and themes that they raise. As a research initiative, this project does, however, seek to be generative of future engagements with architectural curation, and begs the question of how previous models can inform contemporary practices. Perhaps the challenge today is no longer one of resisting the past but rather of affirming its consequences for present and future practice.

Traditionally, the origins of the architecture biennale are thought to officially begin in 1980, when Paolo Portoghesi organised 'The Presence of the Past'. The section titled *Strada Novissima*, in the newly restored Corderie dell'Arsenale, consisted of a series of dramatic facades by leading international architects. The installation provoked a new understanding of Main Street, and is recognised as popularising the postmodern movement in architecture. Its highly theatrical quality – it was constructed with the assistance of craftsmen from the Cinecittà film studios in Rome – continues to serve as a benchmark for subsequent curation. Portoghesi's exhibition also set a precedent in that it was the first to receive international attention from the public, outside of a specialised academic and professional community.

The spectacular success of the *Strada Novissima* has arguably overshadowed the historical importance of other sections of Portoghesi's exhibition, including an exhibition of critics who were commissioned to produce spatial displays, as well as a show, titled 'The Banal Object', on the architect Antonio Basile. Portoghesi's legacy, however, also includes the very space of the Corderie dell'Arsenale, which he had reclaimed in 1980 for purposes of display. In emphasising how an exhibition could directly impact the urban fabric of the city of Venice, Portoghesi created a precedent for the institution itself, one that can be traced through subsequent directors including Francesco Dal Co, who commissioned architect James Stirling to design a new bookstore pavilion in the Giardini for his exhibition in 1991. Through such gestures, Portoghesi and Dal Co remind us that architectural exhibitions are as much about proposals and theoretical lines of enquiry as they are, fundamentally, about building.

In tracing the genealogy of the biennale back even earlier, our project finds that 'Proposition for the Molino Stucky', an exhibition organised in 1975 by Vittorio Gregotti, then director of art and architecture, represents an equally formative development for architecture at the biennale. The exhibition took the form of an international competition regarding the future of the Molino Stucky, an abandoned industrial mill emblematic of the loss of Venice's industrial economy. It was inspired by the role that architects and others can play in urban renewal and it sought to remedy, as Gregotti argued in his catalogue, a 'destiny of exploitation and physical and cultural neglect'.

It was also, fundamentally, an exhibition about social responsiveness, which was a prerequisite of the biennale following its highly politicised opening in 1968. Lawrence Alloway and others have noted how students and intellectuals gathered that year in the Piazza San Marco and at the Giardini in solidarity with geopolitical events around the globe. Artists closed their respective pavilions and turned canvases towards the wall to demand transformations within the institution of the biennale itself, which was accused of being unresponsive to societal developments. With this context in mind, we can understand Carlo Ripa di Meana, the president of the Biennale in 1975, arguing that with Gregotti's exhibition 'an institution like the biennale has, however, a task of its own, to bring culture to bear on administrative decisions, using the modes and idiom of culture'.

How do we reconcile the apparent progressiveness of the Molino Stucky exhibition with the strategic manoeuvres and political calculations that first enabled a forum for architecture at the biennale? As Gregotti and Dal Co both remarked in their conversations with us, contradictions like these define the institution; each project is marked by the reality of complicities and entanglements that each director must accept. In the pages that follow, subsequent directors take up this legacy. They also acknowledge the influence that these incipient models of social responsibility

15

had for their own work and the biennale itself. With these conversations, then, we provide a space in which the plurality of these histories can unfold.

The richness of these early exhibitions, which have only been hinted at here, are indicative of the subtleties inherent in subsequent projects by the biennale directors Francesco Dal Co, Hans Hollein, Massimiliano Fuksas, Deyan Sudjic, Kurt Forster, Richard Burdett, Aaron Betsky and Kazuyo Sejima. Throughout, the self-reflexivity of the directors and their unique responsiveness to their predecessors is particularly evident and serves to enrich our understanding of the biennale as a living institution.

Notably, not a single director of the biennale has received formal curatorial training, which invites reflection on the future of architectural curation at a moment when it is becoming an academic discipline of its own. Inevitably, this project also has a bearing on developments in contemporary art and architecture, and on how the avant-garde is internalised in the institutional structures of biennales, museums and commercial galleries, as well as in alternative spaces and grassroots organisations whose self-definition has traditionally opposed mainstream developments. It calls forth a rethinking of avant-garde engagements with the questioning of authority which have been particularly pronounced throughout the history of the biennale, with the staging of subversive events and the devising of alternative forms of display. This history of experimentation has consequences for a new generation of artists and curators who remain suspended between the unfulfilled aspirations of the historical avant-garde and the complexities and inevitable compromises of contemporary practice.

This project also builds upon William Menking's and my own experience in organising 'Into the Open', the official US representation at the 2008 biennale, with Andrew Sturm. Our project explored the ways American architects today are working collaboratively to invigorate community activism and social policy by mitigating the socio-economic challenges and environmental rifts that define our times. The intention of the project was to question the star-architecture quality of the profession and the privileging of formal invention over socio-political concerns. We sought to enable conversations between architects, policy makers, community leaders and individuals —conversations that we hope have continued even after our last events have been staged. In realising this project, we became attentive to the complexity of presenting exhibitions in such a spectacular venue as the Venice Biennale, where one is inevitably caught between architectures of use and those of display. Just as our exhibition sought to be useful by proposing alternate models of architectural practice, so too the conversations that follow offer other possibilities for curatorial practice. Today, it is not always clear how to display architecture, to whom and for what purpose. By revisiting the articulations featured here, we can perhaps better explore our possibilities. It is in this sense that we see this publication, which seeks to raise more questions than answers, as an appropriately 'open' conclusion to our 2008 project.

In addition to exploring histories of collaboration, this project was itself a collaboration, benefiting from the crucial involvement and assistance of numerous individuals and institutions. At Slought Foundation, this project was part of our 2009/10 research programme; research fellows Melanie Kress, Liana Moskowitz and Megan Schmidgal were instrumental to all aspects of its realisation and were assisted by Tate Obayashi and Scott Jackson. Our sincere thanks goes to Ken Saylor and Prem Krishnamurthy for their intellectual guidance throughout, as well as our friends and colleagues in Venice, Rome, Milan, Philadelphia, New York and London for their hospitality and introductions. We would also like to thank the directors themselves, who have been welcoming and generous with their time and work. Finally, I am indebted to my colleague, mentor and friend William Menking, with whom it has been a pleasure to collaborate on the many intellectual and logistical journeys required to bring this project to reality.

We also acknowledge with gratitude the many institutions, including the US State

Department, the Peggy Guggenheim Collection, PARC Foundation, the Graham Foundation for Advanced Studies in the Fine Arts and *The Architects' Newspaper* among others too numerous to name here, who enabled the 2008 exhibition that provided the germ for this project. We also recognise more recent institutional supporters including the Venice Biennale itself and the Van Alen Institute. Finally, Brett Steele, Stefano Rabolli Pansera, Thomas Weaver, Pamela Johnston and Zak Kyes at the Architectural Association School of Architecture in London have also enabled this project to come to fruition.

Vittorio Gregotti

Milan
Wednesday 16 December 2009

*Vittorio Gregotti directed 'On the Subject of the
Stucky Mill', considered by many to inaugurate an
architectural presence at the Venice Biennale. On
display in 1975 in the Magazzini del Sale at the
Zattere, the exhibition featured design proposals from
artists, architects and local representatives regarding
the future of abandoned granary mills on the Giudecca.
He also directed the 1976 exhibition 'Werkbund
1907' and 'Utopia and the Crisis of Anti-Nature'
in 1978 at the Magazzini del Sale.*

Aaron Levy and William Menking: We're
interested in the origins of the biennale, how it
started. Since you curated the very first exhibitions,
we'd like to know about the kind of things you had
to deal with. We feel that your exhibition at the
Molino Stucky inaugurated a way of presenting
architecture. So could you tell us how it all began
in 1975?

Vittorio Gregotti: Of course, I don't
remember the actual day! It is a strange story.
I was asked to curate the art biennale, which
was traditionally the role of a specialist in
contemporary art. But I was an architect, and

the director of a magazine of architecture, and
no art historian.

WM: So why did they ask an architect?

VG: I don't really know why – it was very
strange. I agreed to do it only if we also had
a small first exhibition of architecture. That
was the condition because if not, well, I wasn't
going to do it. The biennale had never had
an architecture section, so this would be the
first one. We started working on it in 1974,
the exhibition opened in 1975, and the really
important exhibitions followed in the years after
that. It was possible to introduce architecture
into the biennale because it had never been
part of the tradition before, but it was very
difficult to find the space for it because space
is very restricted, of course. The biennale had
been interrupted after the protests of 1968.
I'm sure you're very familiar with the history of
all of this. After this interruption, we started
working again in 1974, with the first exhibition
about the Molino Stucky. It was prepared very
quickly and not very well – it was not a success
in my opinion. In 1976 we started a different
approach to exhibiting architecture. One part
was a historical exhibition, and the other was an
exhibition of modern architecture featuring a
group of Europeans and Americans in order to
compare the two different positions. It was the

time of the New York Five, and in Europe there were two or three different positions, such as Oswald Mathias Ungers in Germany, James Stirling in England, Serge Chermayeff and a few others.

AL: Did you understand at that early moment that you were creating an institution for architecture, a new architectural biennale?

VG: Yes, of course. It was a conscious move, but it was very difficult to work within the existing structure of the biennale, which traditionally had not included architecture – that was the problem.

WM: So you wanted it to be an event every two years, that was part of your idea?

VG: Starting from this moment, yes. The president was changing at the time, but the new president decided that every two years there would be an architecture biennale.

AL: So whereas you saw the Molino Stucky exhibition – a bridge between land art and architecture – as the beginning of the architectural biennale, the administrators of the biennale saw it almost like an extension of the art biennale?

VG: Exactly.

WM: So, precisely because of the history of the art biennale, you approached it in a different kind of way, as an opportunity to present architecture rather than just art?

VG: That's very difficult to answer because it's a critical problem, of course. What is the relationship between art and architecture? For me architecture is an art, so there is no problem. It's not a visual art, but a special field.

WM: And it has its own way of presenting itself, so you could display it in that kind of way.

AL: But it seems that you did more than just involve artists and architects in the Molino Stucky project: you also involved urbanists, builders, inhabitants of the city. It seems that you were trying to be inclusive on a very broad scale.

VG: Of course. But the reason for this exhibition was the problem of 1968. Molino Stucky represents the connection between the ideology of 1968 and after. And that's why it was very political – I wanted to make a clear and certain declaration that the biennale was open to the public, to Venice and to non-specialists.

WM: Do you think your exhibition contributed to, and maybe determined, the biennale's subsequent course?

VG: I think so. I think the biennale, rightly or not, has become very important to the field of architecture, to the larger biennale, to Venice and to Italy as a whole.

AL: I want to return to your Molino Stucky exhibition. You mentioned that in a sense it was a political manoeuvre. You made a political calculation by involving artists, architects and the inhabitants of the city, in this way creating a competition of ideas. But you were also interested in the very real future of the Molino Stucky – in the future of the city itself. The Molino Stucky, after all, is now a luxury Hilton hotel: it has been transformed from an abandoned flour mill into a tourist site.

VG: Yes, it has changed completely. The problems that the city of Venice faces are complicated, and very difficult to address. We never think to speak about these problems. In the case of the Molino Stucky, of course, it was different.

AL: You mean it was not meant as a polemic but rather as a symbolic gesture towards the idea of social engagement?

VG: Yes, of course. There was also a strategy concerning the relationship between visual art and architecture. That was really the beginning of this idea for the exhibition. With the next exhibition, in 1976, there was only a small number of internationally known architects at that time, so in a sense the choice was easy. Now the choice is practically impossible, and this is the problem. I tried to discuss the exhibition with the representatives of all the different nations. This was very difficult because every nation was completely independent.

AL: In his remarks in the Molino Stucky catalogue the biennale president, Carlo Ripa di Meana, explains that he hopes that the project – by involving artists and architects – would influence the institution. Was that the stance he had to take following 68?

VG: Of course. Afterwards, his position changed completely.

WM: I want to go back to your earlier remarks and understand one thing. In 1975 you organised the Molino Stucky exhibition at the Magazzini del Sale, yet you said that the following year's 'Werkbund' exhibition was for you the real biennale. 'Utopia and the Crisis of Anti-Nature' took place two years later in 1978. These exhibitions unfolded over three years, but you thought of them in a way as a single project. It was all part of the same thing.

VG: The problem was to convince all of the people overseeing the biennale, as well as those coming to the biennale and representing regions, states, etc. In effect, three years passed before the first real exhibition of architecture.

AL: It's interesting that the process now is so different to how things were done then. But you were doing it because you were trying to convince the administration that they needed to have this?

VG: Exactly. Now it is completely different, because the president makes the decisions very quickly and easily.

WM: The other thing that is surely different is the amount of money now available – a lot of euros are required today to make it all happen!

VG: That is another problem, the problem of money. At the time we were in Venice, it was absolutely impossible. Practically all my assistants arrived without money, they paid their own way.

WM: And the architects featured in the exhibition also paid to come and be involved?

VG: Yes, but it was a very special moment because of their enthusiasm, and also their friendship with me and the other architects.

WM: How many people came to it, and could you tell if it was a success? The newspapers and everybody talked about it?

VG: No, it was only ever in the specialist and trade journals. It did not have a popular, mass appeal.

AL: But you assumed that its effect would be registered in years to come?

VG: Yes.

AL: And the publication for the Molino Stucky exhibition, when did it appear?

VG: I think it was a few months later. It was a very modest catalogue. Now each year they produce an enormous monument of a catalogue – very large, very important.

AL: The political compromises you made at the time seem to be a necessary response to the circumstances you found yourself in. Today, we have so many of our own problems and compromises. What were some of the other problems that you remember having? You just spoke of the financial difficulties, and you have alluded to difficulties in convincing the administration to do it.

VG: We of course had numerous discussions

with the Venetian administration, and presented ourselves as allied to the Communist Party over the Christian Party – but political divisions and interests were much clearer then.

AL: Did the participants then understand the importance of what they were part of? And did they see it as an architectural exhibition, which is how we remember it now?

VG: My strategy was to downplay it and suggest that the whole thing was not especially important. Today, though, I really feel that the current biennales are not so interesting. Of course, the problem of information is completely different today compared to the 1970s, but the position of different architects is not made clear – I think things are very complicated, very confused, not only in relation to art but also within architecture. With Portoghesi's biennale, I was completely against postmodern architecture, but it was a position, that's for sure. Then there was postmodern and there was modern. At this moment, what is the position? It's impossible to know. Since Portoghesi, there is no real discussion taking place. But I understand very well why that's happening, because regardless of whether it is right or wrong, the general situation in architecture is like everything else in the world today.

AL: It is not the fault of the biennale that it is this way, but at the same time you would hope that the biennale would enable us to achieve some clarity or direction?

VG: Yes, for us and for architecture. Because of the market, the problem today is simply knowing who are the new artists. The same goes for architecture.

WM: Had there been an architectural presence in the art biennale before 1975?

VG: No, not really. There were some architects – Scarpa for example – who were involved in the biennale, its buildings and exhibition designs, but in general architects did not have much of a presence.

WM: But the triennale in Milan had a long history of involving architecture...

VG: Oh, that's another story altogether, a completely different history. The triennale started before the 1930s outside Milan. It was an exhibition of interior design. It came to Milan in 1934 and began to become a real biennale of modern architecture. After 1945 it again changed completely, becoming an exhibition that included everything – design, fashion, interior design and a little bit of architecture. In the 1960s I was part of Gruppo T, which was composed essentially of philosophers, poets, two or three artists, one or two musicians and me as an architect. We decided to occupy the triennale and made an exhibition on the theme of leisure, the free time after work. And in 1964 I was appointed curator of the triennale.

WM: Was the triennale closely aligned with industry at that time?

VG: Not much, only ideologically speaking.

WM: So why did you go to Venice when you could have continued your work there? Was it because of the rich history of the biennale and it being associated with art at the time? Because if you could already do things at the triennale, why not just continue to curate architecture exhibitions at the Milan triennale?

VG: I was not the director of the triennale. I was its curator in 1964 and that was the end of it. Every triennale had a different curator, of course, and back then it did not feature art or architecture, just interior design.

AL: So for you, the triennale didn't serve as a model for Venice. Venice was supposed to be something entirely different?

VG: Yes.

WM: And that's because Venice already held a very different position in the world, a different tradition at the time.

VG: Yes, completely different. The biennale first started in 1895, while the triennale effectively started in 1930. It's very important to note the relationship with the triennale, because I think it's an important element for Italian culture, and of course also for international culture. In the 1930s the triennale also started with international pavilions, or sections, for Austria, for Germany, for France, etc. My participation in the triennale was important, too, for my nomination to the biennale.

AL: Bill and I have difficulty knowing how to show architecture today, because it seems that it is no longer sufficient to put the plan or the model on the wall.

VG: It's absolutely impossible. For me, that's the real elemental difficulty of having an exhibition of architecture. Communication with the public is practically impossible.

AL: Is this a perennial problem for you or something particular to today?

VG: It's a problem specific to today. Before there were no problems with the public, the discussion was only among specialists. Now the pretension of the biennale is to involve the people, not just architects or artists, and that's practically impossible. That's what I think anyway, maybe it's not the case.

AL: I'm interested to know if you'd argue that your exhibition was itself a creative work?

VG: *Sì, sì.*

Paolo Portoghesi

Calcata
Saturday 19 December 2009

Paolo Portoghesi directed the first and second architecture exhibitions at the Venice Biennale. The first, 'The Presence of the Past', in 1980 in the Corderie dell'Arsenale, encompassed a variety of exhibition practices, including exhibitions about twentieth-century architectural masters; the Strada Novissima installation, which staged a lively debate around postmodern approaches to architecture; and the construction of Aldo Rossi's Teatro del Mondo. The second, 'Architecture in Islamic Countries', in 1982 in the Padiglione Italia at the Giardini, explored the influence of Islamic architectural culture in modernity and the role of architecture in providing a meeting point between western and eastern cultures.

Aaron Levy and William Menking: We're interested in the history of your *Strada Novissima* exhibit. When we spoke with Gregotti regarding his Molino Stucky exhibition of 1975, he seemed to anticipate its future impact. Did you understand at the time how important your exhibition would be, not only giving the architecture biennale a greater visibility internationally, but also offering a model for the display of architecture?

Paolo Portoghesi: Gregotti was the director of the two exhibitions that preceded mine, and he certainly made exhibitions dedicated to architecture, but after Gregotti the biennale wanted to create something new – a new section parallel to the exhibitions of visual arts. So I was the director of the first international architecture exhibition, and it was pretty successful because it travelled to Paris and San Francisco. The idea was not to show images of architecture, but to show real architecture. My idea was to make something close to reality that accommodated the various interpretations of symbolic architecture set out by the architects. At the same time, I put in a request to use the Corderie dell'Arsenale as a space for the biennale. When I visited the place it was still full of tanks and armaments. It was very difficult to persuade the Italian military to move them, but in the end we were successful. This was a very important step, because without the space of the Corderie it would have been impossible to create an exhibition featuring three-dimensional architecture.

AL: Did you think of the renovation of the Corderie as part of the ideology of your exhibition, or as just a necessary first step?

PP: I considered the Arsenale to be the only really useful space for my biennale. Because it's very close to the Giardini, it was also a natural expansion of the exhibition towards the centre of the city. In addition to the Corderie, many other parts of Venice were used as well. As you know, the biennale is separated from Venice, and there has often been a conflict between the Venetians and the biennales, which is very strange. So I tried to create a new situation of cooperation between institutions, and I thought it was very important to locate the biennale more centrally in the city.

WM: One of the things Gregotti said was that there was not much of a public at the biennale when he started – it was just him and people he knew. The architectural world was very small at that point, and those who attended were people who were already interested in the biennale. In your opinion, did you feel that it was popular with the public or not? Was it a closed world like that?

PP: I think Gregotti's view of the biennale was somewhat elitist – I wanted to create something popular. With architecture there is always the possibility of direct communication between people and architects. Architecture for architects, accordingly, is wrong, and it breaks the continuity of architectural history. Architecture is not for architects – it's for the public. I believe that modern architecture has lost the capacity to speak to the citizens, the common people.

For example, Gregotti curated an exhibition on *macchine celibi* (singular machines) – a show that I consider totally inappropriate. I think architecture is not like the visual arts. A picture can simply be shown, but architecture is something that imposes its presence on people. The fact that my exhibition was in a certain sense connected to postmodernism has led it to be misinterpreted. The idea of postmodernism, in relation to the exhibition, was generated by Charles Jencks, who was present in the commission. He was a friend, but his approach was very different. In Europe postmodernism is associated with the spectacular, the superficial. I was more interested in the Venturi experience.

WM: Main Street, as we call it.

PP: Yes. I consider Venturi to be a kindred spirit. There is something similar in my own approach to architecture. He was in Rome in the 1950s, and to me the lesson of Rome is a lesson of humility. Venturi very sensibly recognised this. This is quite different to Rome as understood by Le Corbusier and others.

WM: What else was in your biennale besides the *Strada Novissima*? Was anything exhibited in the Italian pavilion? And what was 'The Exhibition of Critics'?

PP: In the Arsenale, at the end of the Via Novissima, there was this space in which Jencks installed a big pencil and Norberg-Schulz made a diorama dedicated to architecture history.

AL: Francesco Dal Co and current biennale president Paolo Baratta have spoken of the importance of using the space of the Corderie theatrically. Baratta in particular spoke of the importance of the curator creating tableaus. Were you attempting something similar with your *Strada Novissima*? Were you trying to formulate or advocate a spectacular, theatrical or perhaps even cinematic manner of displaying architecture?

PP: Many critics have spoken of the cinematic quality of the *Strada Novissima*. My idea, originally, was to make a real model of a street – to replicate the condition of all Italian cities, and of competition between architects, in order to create a social space, one that allowed for the harmony of different architectural practices. Certainly, the result was cinematic. For the architects, it was perhaps a gallery of self-portraits, and this is probably also the reason for its success. But I consider it positive in this respect, because cinematography is useful in reconnecting citizens with architecture. So for me this critique was a kind of compliment. For me the Via Novissima was an illusion, but at the same time a big success.

AL: Did you envision the *Strada Novissima*, insofar as it sought to reconnect citizens with architecture, as a prototype for subsequent biennales?

PP: You know that the director who came directly after me was Aldo Rossi, and Rossi was a protagonist in my biennale – I made an effort to demonstrate to him the possibilities of the exhibition just as Gregotti had done for me. The biennale provided me with an opportunity to present a different way of connecting modern architecture with history, and gradually Rossi accepted my invitation to participate. He didn't want to design a facade on the *Strada Novissima*, but he did design the entrance to the entire exhibition. This was typical of Aldo. In the Teatro del Mondo that we constructed for the 1980 biennale there was also an exhibition of Aldo's works. We made this space together with Maurizio Scaparro, director of the theatrical section of the biennale. After my exhibitions of 1980 and 1982 Rossi accepted the directorship, but there was a battle inside the biennale. I had become president by then and I wanted to give the directorship to Rossi because he made exhibitions that invited architects to give something back to Venice through projects, photo-assignments and various services, but many other people in the administration wanted to make Renzo Piano the next director. So the idea to create architecture that would outlast the exhibition was common both to Rossi and Dal Co, and it has given the biennale a closer relationship with Venice. It should also be noted that Dal Co did something very important, strengthening the connection between the structures of the art and architecture biennales by involving foreign states and official commissions.

AL: Was the participation of the national pavilions something you hoped to achieve in 1980, or was that not what you were interested in?

PP: We organised this exhibition in a very short time, so it just wasn't possible. I was nominated director in January, by March we had already made Rossi's Teatro del Mondo, and in August or September the biennale opened.

WM: We have been told that you brought workers from Cinecittà in Rome to build the *Strada Novissima*. Is this true?

PP: It was the only way to create it in such a short time! All of the workers had made moulds and structures, so they were able very rapidly to create the illusion we were seeking.

WM: And it then travelled to San Francisco?

PP: We brought it to San Francisco because

there was a fantastic lady who was very motivated and who loved the exhibition and wanted it there. Philip Johnson was the sponsor. It was in Fort Mason, a site that is very similar to the Arsenale in a way.

AL: But Johnson was also in the biennale? Was it true that you made the *Presence of the Past* in homage to Johnson, as well as Mario Ridolfi and Ignazio Gardella?

PP: In homage to Johnson, yes, but also to Ridolfi and Gardella who were for me exemplary architects of modernity. I was very interested in their connection with history and their respect for place, for a kind of popular culture. This was the real ideological basis for the exhibition. The idea was that they were outside critics who were inside the modern movement and not connected with the traditionalism that typified most Italian culture. They were courageous figures who created a rationalist architecture that was connected to local traditions. Gardella's Dispensario Antitubercolare in Alessandria, for instance, was rationalist but at the same time connected with popular, humble traditions.

WM: Where did you study architecture? Who were your professors?

PP: In Rome. As a teacher I went to Milan, during the period of unrest. I was suspended for my solidarity with the students, along with Aldo Rossi, Franco Albini and Guido Canella among others. We were suspended from teaching for three years!

AL: What was the 'Banal Object', the show that was also part of your biennale in 1980?

PP: To get into the Via Novissima you had to pass through the Banal Object, an exhibition on the work of the architect Antonio Basile. For me it was important for the biennale to show some historical exhibitions, and I considered Basile to be an important part of Italian history. This was very rich material that had never been exposed. Italy is a special part of Europe where modernity was accepted with conditions. Basile accepted it completely but within a Sicilian tradition. It was a biennale typical of the Italian contribution to modernity – which always has some condition attached. And that is the problem of Italy.

AL: Was there anything that you learned from the exhibition? I suppose I am thinking in particular of the *Strada Novissima*.

PP: Oh yes, I learned that it was difficult to be understood!

AL: Even with that one, which was perhaps the clearest of all the exhibitions on architecture?

PP: Yes. I also learned that when something is successful, there is something wrong with it.

AL: But you wanted to provoke with the exhibition, right? That was the very idea?

PP: I was against a certain type of conformity typical of the early 1980s, which adopted the form of a style without also absorbing its value and its quality. So this exhibition was a provocation related to that. Sometimes in Italy the idea is to imitate what is happening outside, and this imitation was being done badly.

AL: You became president of the biennale just after this?

PP: Yes, I became president due to the wave of success of the exhibition. The first four years were very interesting for me, and the second four were terrible. In the first four years the visual art exhibitions (in 1986 and 1988) were the best of the biennale. In the second four years there were many difficulties, because the financial resources of the biennale only stretched to paying for the salaries. So trying to organise in this position was completely dangerous.

AL: You also organised the biennale on Islamic architecture in 1982?

PP: This was the second exhibition that I undertook as director. I think it was important because it represented a spirit of cultural dialogue. The Islamic architects presented many interesting projects.

WM: Why did you choose that particular subject at that particular moment? Was it because of the richness of the work being done that was unknown in the West?

PP: I was very interested in having a dialogue with the Islamic people. I considered this very important for peace, for avoiding a war of religions. Bear in mind that I had just completed the competition for the Islamic mosque in Rome in 1974.

WM: One of the things we talked about with Gregotti and Dal Co was the degree to which a biennale should reflect contemporary culture or alternatively lead that culture. With the Islamic show you were really trying to direct the culture, to do something provocative. I imagine it wasn't a particularly popular subject in 1982.

PP: The exhibition of Islamic architecture was very interesting because there was no

modernist movement in Islamic countries –
instead, modern architecture arrived through
colonialism. Now it's finished, but that moment
was very interesting to observe because
the situation was so different from the one
in Europe. The exhibition attracted many
visitors, probably because the biennale had by
then begun to reach international eyes. This
international character has really expanded, and
the biennale is now important for international
architects. It is fantastic to see so many young
people come. It is also a big responsibility.

AL: I don't know if you were thinking this way at
the time, but did you think of the 1980 exhibition
as a curatorial project or as an aesthetic project in
itself?

PP: In my life I have only made exhibitions for
the biennale. Making exhibitions is generally
not my thing – my preferred work is to design.
But I remember the biennale as being a very
interesting point in my life, especially when I
return to Venice.

AL: Do you continue to attend the biennales today?

PP: I think the last interesting biennale was
the one directed by Hans Hollein. After that,
I think the shows haven't offered any special
contribution. Giving architects a statistical

idea of the role of the citizen in the world is not useful, it's not indicative of the beauty of the biennale, which is about artistic culture. Sejima's show will certainly be more interesting. It will be a return to the duty of the biennale, which is to manifest what is happening in the *culture* of the world.

AL: Was it easy to convince the architects to participate in the *Strada Novissima* and the *Presence of the Past*?

PP: It was not easy to convince Robert Venturi to be present. The same with Aldo Rossi. It was Scully especially who convinced Robert to participate. Gehry too was unsure about the project, and certainly against the idea. After he arrived in Venice he decided not to participate, for the reason that the facade was too simple. I convinced him to take part in the end, and his turned out to be one of the more interesting facades, and one that had a critical meaning. In a certain sense, his was more close to my idea. In the Gehry facade was the memory of American architecture, something original in the sense of an essence, a tradition.

Francesco Dal Co

Venice
Wednesday 16 December 2009

Francesco Dal Co directed the fifth architecture exhibition at the Venice Biennale, on display from 8 September to 6 October 1991 in the Corderie dell'Arsenale, the Padiglione Italia and the national pavilions at the Giardini. Besides an exhibition on the role of education in architecture, the biennale was notable for the commissioning of a new bookshop pavilion designed by James Stirling and the encouragement of international participation.

Aaron Levy and William Menking: You were part of Gregotti's committee in 1975 for the Molino Stucky project. So before we get to the biennale that you yourself directed, we wanted to begin by asking you to tell us what you remember of that period, and what your involvement was.

Francesco Dal Co: After 1968 the biennale was closed for some time. When it reopened around 1975, the structure of the entire institution had changed, but they did keep the directors, and it was now their job to do everything. For this reason, Gregotti was running both art and architecture. It was mandatory to have one committee for art and another for architecture, and I was on the committee for architecture. The 1975 show was an attempt on our part to establish the idea that the architecture biennale could have the same status as – and compete with – the art biennale. The administrative structure was very different from now. There was a rather gigantic board of administrators, around 20 to 25 people, who made the general decisions. The role of the director at the time was very important, something which is not true anymore, in part because there is very little time to prepare. Today, the directors work for a few months and they rely a lot on the president of the biennale who has become a kind of general manager organising everything. I had much more power than a director does now. But this power was inversely related to the amount of money I had available. That was the big problem! One of my big achievements was to convince foreign countries to invest money in the biennale. In the beginning we didn't even open the Giardini and the pavilions. The administrators at the time made that decision, because they were somehow afraid that reopening them would lead to trouble. So we started to open new spaces in the city instead. The idea was to use the biennale as a tool to recuperate spaces in the town. In 1975 we opened the biennale in the Magazzini del Sale, the national building. When Portoghesi was appointed as director (before he became president) he had the great idea of opening the Corderie. This was arguably the most important thing he did.

AL: In a certain sense, in your biennale as well as Portoghesi's, you attempted not just to show architecture but to rehabilitate and renovate infrastructure.

FDC: We were convinced that one of the priorities of the architectural biennale should be to create exhibitions that would have a different relationship to the spaces themselves, and provide new opportunities to do things. This came from the first experience with the Molino Stucky in 1975, and from what Portoghesi did with the *Strada Novissima* and the great success he enjoyed when he gave the Teatro del Mondo to Aldo Rossi to design.

AL: How was the Corderie used in your case?

FDC: When I arrived we had 330m of the Corderie to use for the first time, but a budget of practically zero. (There must be ten times more money available now.) So we came up with the idea of inviting schools of architecture from all over the world to participate, and it turned out to be very successful. Portoghesi had opened new spaces and taken over the Giardini. When I arrived, I understood that this was going to be very difficult to do – again, because we had no money. And so I started to think that it was time to invest new energy in improving the Giardini. We had received several requests from several countries that wanted to build their own pavilion. This was difficult to do, both administratively and because of the restrictions in Venice. So I decided to send a different message with the building of the bookshop by James Stirling, which became a similar kind of event to Rossi's Teatro del Mondo. But the difference was that the bookshop was not a temporary building. It was permanent, and it was inside the Giardini. I was interested in having the presence of a very new building, and not just a Cinecittà object as with Portoghesi or Rossi. This was also an attempt on my part to demonstrate that it was possible to satisfy the requests we had received from foreign countries at this time.

WM: We have a couple more questions based on our conversation with Gregotti. He at one point said that it was a project of his to bring architecture to Venice. Also, I wondered if the politics after 68 meant that architecture had somehow to engage in urban issues?

FDC: I think the architectural biennale was the by-product of the growing interest in architecture in general, and of the fact that there was an extremely lively school in Venice at the time. It was a real place for international confrontations. Just a few years before the biennale, there was a very famous seminar with Aldo Rossi, Rafael Moneo and Peter Eisenman.

AL: Was the political climate something that influenced what Gregotti or you yourself did in your own exhibitions?

FDC: We were thinking at that time in terms of possibilities for confronting art and architectural experiences. The board of administrators were political people. They were representatives of the dominant political parties, the trade unions and other interests. Generally this is very unhealthy for an institution, but for us it was extremely beneficial, because while they were busy fighting with each other we could get on and do what we wanted.

WM: And was Molino Stucky just a competition with young people and students to rethink the building?

FDC: I know that we were interested in encouraging people to come to Venice to study the problems of the city, and to use those problems to create the occasion for a project. Aldo Rossi for instance did a competition for the bridge of the l'Accademia. This was an approach that all of us Italians shared – Vittorio, Aldo, myself, etc – and it has been lost completely. When I was director, I would speak directly with the ministers of culture of different countries. I even had the direct telephone number of the Italian Prime Minister. Now, it's a different situation. In my time, the director was the person, now it's the manager or the president who has that authority.

WM: Gregotti told us that in the beginning the people who went to the biennale were intellectuals, specialists and friends, and it wasn't as open to the general public. But that changed with the *Strada Novissima* and of course goes on today.

FDC: Yes, it has changed a lot since then. But the transformation is not only due to the biennale itself. You wouldn't believe how this city changed after the collapse of the Berlin Wall, for instance. Now we have 20 million visitors each year!

AL: I wasn't sure, but I got the impression that Gregotti seemed almost to wish that the biennale could still be addressed to a specialist community.

FDC: I think that the nature of our society is changing. You have to respond to these changes and try to find a way in which an institution like the biennale can improve general tastes and help people to understand and learn more. It is a wider problem of our age. When I started working at the biennale it was a totally different time. All the guys working for me had been there since the 1930s, and only a few countries were represented. Today, the whole of Venice is filled with pavilions. The furniture fair in Milan was in my time also a very simple fair, now it has transformed the very use of an entire section of the city. And what can you do? It's bad and it's wrong, but this is the situation we have to live with.

WK: Have you enjoyed the last couple of biennales? Do you find them compelling?

FDC: They asked me to go back to being director after my four years, and I had to say, 'I don't want do it again, please try new people.' It's an experience you can only do once, because you will inevitably repeat yourself. Likewise, I never answer the question about whether I like a particular biennale. I have seen so many! Some are better than others, but each one offers a chance to see something interesting.

AL: In some histories of the architecture biennale your biennale is the fifth, but then in another sense it could be argued that it's the first, because it was the first one to involve the national pavilions.

FDC: Yes, this was a discussion at the time. But I prefer to say that it is the fifth. I had always the perception that we started with Vittorio's. I was the first one to involve all the pavilions, but it's the fifth biennale overall.

AL: So Vittorio's was understood at the time as being the first articulation, or did this idea arise afterwards?

FDC: Afterwards. The idea that there were five biennales came with my biennale. They said, 'This is the first biennale of architecture', and I said, 'No, it's the biennale that comes after Vittorio, Paolo and Aldo.' But I would avoid the conclusion that Vittorio, Paolo, Aldo and myself invented this. We were just reacting to what was suggested at the time. When Vittorio organised his triennale in Milan in 1964 it was the best moment of Milanese culture. Umberto Eco was there, and all the architects were extremely alive. It was the time when Giò Ponti was so important, and Ignazio Gardella was there, Franco Albini too. But to say that Vittorio was inventing something in organising that triennale is in my opinion wrong. You can be the interpreter of something, and to be sure Vittorio had his ideas. But why was the biennale so important at that time, why is it so important today? It is because it is the expression of a culture and atmosphere of the time.

AL: But you were also each actively shifting or transforming the institution's identity. In 1991, for instance, you undertook the James Stirling project, which I understand was continuing a new tradition of renovation and rehabilitation. By including the national pavilions for the first time, weren't you trying to set a precedent, invent a trajectory?

FDC: Yes, I had always been convinced that the big difference between the biennale and all the other institutions is the foreign pavilions, and that getting greater national participation in the pavilions was the most important problem from the cultural point of view. There used to be an interesting national tradition at the Giardini: when the artist first arrived at the pavilion a flag representing their nation would go up. I always thought that this was a very important message of respect, and not just something with symbolic meaning.

AL: So that was a sort of forgotten tradition that you restored for that one year.

FDC: Yes, just for 1991.

WK: We feel that in a way the biennale is in danger of losing a sense of intimacy in an age when everything is becoming mutable and digital. Information is passed around the world so quickly now. Is it possible that the biennale, despite its importance today, could end up being less crucial to the exchange of ideas and information? Today everybody knows everything, and in a way they seem to know it before they get there.

FDC: I think it is a danger, you're right. The first change is the way in which organisations are run. If you're short of time, you just make a few phone calls and people send stuff, and you end up with nothing more than a vitrine, a shop window. The profession has also changed a lot since 1976, when architects would come and stay here for months. If they were very well known, they might have been a bit reluctant, but they were not as busy as they are now. Today it's difficult. They have to keep an eye on their work, they have offices with tons of people working for them. Another thing that has changed is the way we articulate our ideas. When you were expressing a clear idea, you used to assume that you would have to fight for it. Today, everyone is looking for consensus, for approval.

AL: The *Strada Novissima* made spectacular use of the exhibition space, presenting architecture in a very dynamic way. But it also set a very difficult precedent – one that everybody coming after, including yourself, has had to live with.

FDC: When Paolo did the *Strada Novissima*

it generated a lot of controversy. Some people said that architecture is theatre, others that architecture is not theatre, and so on. His idea was brilliant and very spectacular, but it was completely fake, and it was built by the same people who built the Cinecittà in Rome. I met the guys, and they can build anything in a short time. It was great theatrical scenery: it had no logical structure, but it stood up nonetheless.

WK: Did it run the whole length of the Arsenale?

FDC: No, it only went through one third of the Corderie, because there was no money to open the whole thing, and also because the Corderie was filled with garbage. Military equipment had been abandoned there since the First World War! So cleaning it up was not just a matter of sweeping something away. You had to transfer gigantic machines, tanks and guns off site.

AL: Can you speak more about your biennale?

FDC: Well, I was pretty sure of two things. One was that I had to have an object, a statement, about the direction it was taking. And the second, which was different from what other directors had done, was to reinvent some forgotten or unknown episodes of the past. For instance, I arranged for the Pikionis exhibition in the Greek pavilion. Millions of people walk up to the Acropolis, and Pikionis is the man who designed the area around the Parthenon. But nobody knows that it was his work! This was for me the most important thing about my biennale, and it was an extraordinary success. This was a statement.

WK: So you had influence over the national pavilions, then? You engaged them in conversation?

FDC: Yes, this was precisely the role I had, which is no longer the case with the current directors.

WK: What do you think of the current interest in displaying architectural ideas through installations?

FDC: If you create an exhibition with real objects, starting from drawings, models and pictures, you have to do a lot of work to tell the complex history of each building. You have to think carefully about the way in which you exhibit. If you just put up a lot of televisions instead, well it's fast and boring. Everything becomes the same, interchangeable. Our displays were still influenced by Carlo Scarpa, who had installed many exhibitions at the biennale. Vittorio, Paolo, Aldo and myself, we were aware of what he used to do, and so when we installed our exhibitions we always thought about how he might have done it.

We gave a great deal of attention to the problem of presenting exhibitions, and I think this aspect is completely unknown to those who have come after us. I'm not saying that my age was better, just that it's different.

AL: It's interesting to hear that Scarpa served as such an influence, if not a structuring device, for your own installations.

FDC: I didn't want to do a Scarpa installation, obviously, but I wanted everyone to understand what they were exhibiting and what they wanted to communicate with it. I don't know if I was always successful, but this was my aim. You might agree with Scarpa or not, say that he's good or not good, but when you saw his temporary and permanent installations you would see the art of arranging an exhibition. He continually offered you something. With this critical gesture, he said: please, look at this. This object is different from that. And these gestures are something that we have lost.

AL: And these gestures do not necessarily have to be visually splendid or spectacular, you are saying?

FDC: No, you can do it with the most simple and obvious things.

AL: Today there is such an acute desire on the part

of the public for something spectacular, something visually enticing.

FDC: Look, the *Strada Novissima* was just as spectacular, but in a very different way. Aldo's Teatro del Mondo is the same. When you see those photos of it next to the Salute, where I guess it was docked, it just seems so incredible. It was emblematic of Venice but it really stood apart.

AL: I want to return to your 1991 exhibition and specifically to the central role it gave to education and pedagogy. When you invited 43 schools to participate, was this because you felt that the biennale could play a role in architectural education, and that the Italian model wasn't working?

FDC: I wanted to offer an opportunity for students to understand how an architect becomes an architect. Today, everyone comes to Venice, sees a building by Zaha Hadid, and thinks she was born an architect. But she was first a mathematician. So I wanted to show the differences in approach and style across different institutions. I was also interested to see what could happen when regions that are not usually in the spotlight were given a chance to shine. For the first time, we showed and worked with kids from China, New Zealand, Australia and so on, which have very lively, healthy cultures. The other aspect that was important to this project was that the students lived here for one month. The formula was very simple. We gave them a small amount of money, helped them find places to stay and offered them basic technical tools to create whatever they wanted to create. But it was mandatory for them to participate in everything. It was really a great experience and some of them now are famous architects. We transformed the Corderie into a gigantic laboratory for a month!

AL: I have a few last questions. If I understand correctly, the first 'official' participation by the United States in your architecture biennale was not entirely official. Instead, it was undertaken independently by Philip Johnson. Is that correct? It is nearly impossible to find documentation about this.

FDC: This is a funny story. The American pavilion didn't have money, and for some reason they didn't want to invest money. So I spoke with my friends in America and said, 'This is stupid, you have to do something.' I had known Philip for many years, and so I spoke to him and explained everything. And he said 'let me think about it'. The next day he called back and said 'I have an idea, I have money from Knoll and I want to invite Peter Eisenman and Frank Gehry.' And I said, 'Fantastic. You do the

exhibition, you are the curator.' And he s
aid okay. But afterwards he sent me a fax saying
that he wanted to be the official curator. And
I thought, how can I do it? It's the American
pavilion, we have no power to say you are the
curator. Then I thought, who cares. And I took
my best stationery, which proclaimed that I
was the director of the biennale, and I wrote a
letter that officially stated: 'I nominate you the
curator of the American pavilion.' Philip was
happy, and nobody discussed it again.

AL: And what are your thoughts about the
1996 show in the US pavilion exploring Disney
Corporation architecture? If I understand correctly,
this was also undertaken without official support.
Do you agree that it was a very fascinating and
appropriate show for Venice?

FDC: I think that it was interesting because
it was kind of looking ahead to this age we
are living in now. It was kind of a preview
to what would happen today: first Disney,
afterwards Dubai.

Hans Hollein

New York
Saturday 15 May 2010

Hans Hollein directed 'Sensing the Future: The Architect as Seismograph', the sixth architecture exhibition at the Venice Biennale. The exhibition, on display from 15 September to 17 November 1996 in the Padiglione Italia and the national pavilions at the Giardini, explored the architect's role in determining architectural futures, building on recent technological developments.

Aaron Levy and William Menking: Our questions for you today concern 'Sensing the Future: The Architect as Seismograph', the biennale for architecture that you directed in 1996.

Hans Hollein: I was the first non-Italian director of the biennale in 1996, but my participation as an artist went back to 1972, with my installation in the Austrian pavilion. Then I was commissioner of the Austrian pavilion of the architecture biennale in 1988, as well as in 1991 with '13 Austrian Positions', in 1996 with 'Coop Himmelb(l)au' and 'Visionary Architecture', in 2000 with 'Austria – Area of Action for International Architects', and in 2001 with 'Area of Tolerance'. I was also

the commissioner of the Austrian pavilion
for every art biennale from 1978 to 1990.
For example, I organised exhibitions on Arnulf
Rainer in 1978, Valie Export in 1980 and
Franz West in 1990.

WM: It's very interesting that you have participated
in and directed the biennale both as an artist and
as an architect. When we look back to the very
beginning of the biennale, the question of what
distinguishes the art and the architecture biennales
is somewhat less clear, even confusing.

HH: Not for me.

AL: Weren't you in Portoghesi's *Strada Novissima*
in 1980?

HH: Yes, I was featured in the *Strada
Novissima* and in Portoghesi's later exhibition
'Architecture: Modernity and the Sacred Space',
which was held in 1992 on the Giudecca.

AL: So you were the first non-Italian director of the
architecture biennale. What was that like and what
problems did you encounter as a result?

HH: Well, it was a very complicated thing.
The biennale has changed since 1996, but at
that time it was a state endeavour and wasn't
open to private financing. Even when people

wanted to give me money, the state wouldn't allow it. However, by the time of Fuksas' biennale in 2000, it was no longer strictly a state operation. There is an interesting story about my appointment as the first non-Italian director. I am a professor in Austria, and as a professor in Austria I am a public servant. As the director of the biennale I was also an Italian public servant. I needed to apply for a permit in Austria to let me do both.

WM: It's interesting that they allowed you at a fairly early date to pick non-Austrians for the Austrian pavilion. This is not yet the case with the United States pavilion, where there is still an expectation that the featured artists or architects should be from the US.

AL: Who were the major international architects that you featured in the Padiglione Italia at the 1996 biennale?

HH: I showed the work of many architects including Frank Gehry, Tadao Ando, Jean Nouvel, Renzo Piano, Zaha Hadid, Coop Himmelb(l)au, Peter Eisenman, Norman Foster, Herzog & de Meuron, Arata Isozaki, Toyo Ito, Philippe Starck, Jørn Utzon, Alvaro Siza, Massimiliano Fuksas, Rem Koolhaas and Rafael Moneo. I had demanded the freedom to select whoever I wanted. With selections such as these, you often get, every other day, a message from someone saying: 'you should put so-and-so in the show!'

AL: What about the Golden Lions for architecture that you awarded that year, and the special awards that you gave for architectural photography?

HH: The Golden Lion was associated with film and had never been given in architecture before. I didn't agree that only actors and filmmakers should get Golden Lions, so I created a Golden Lion award for architecture as well. The first Golden Lions for architecture were given to three people: Ignazio Gardella, Philip Johnson and Oscar Niemeyer. They were 89, 90 and 91 years old at the time! For the first time, I also organised an exhibition of architectural photography. It was a joint collaboration between photographer Gabriele Basilico and architect Stefano Boeri. And I gave Basilico a special award as well. However, I don't believe later directors continued this.

WM: Could you talk a little bit about your specific ideas for your show? Recent curators like Aaron Betsky, Ricky Burdett or Deyan Sudjic have all had a theme, be it cities, demographics or even the return to building. Did you have a particular series of ideas at the time about presenting architecture in a certain way?

HH: Sure. Otherwise I wouldn't have done it! The idea was to show how the architect is like a seismograph, sensing the future. In contrast to earlier biennales, most of the pavilions chimed in with a related presentation on this general topic.

WM: Do you recall what the American pavilion exhibited that year?

HH: There was an exhibition about the Disney Corporation and its architectural patronage of the avant-garde. I made Tom Krens the commissioner because the Americans couldn't decide themselves. Most other countries have a Ministry of Culture that takes charge, but the set up with the United States is different. So I went and gave them a kind of ultimatum and said: 'You have to come up with something, otherwise you cannot participate.'

WM: So Tom Krens made the decision to focus on Disney?

HH: Yes, which was okay.

WM: To return to your exhibition, you included some architects in the 'Emerging Voices' show that you had individually picked. Could you talk a little bit about that? It turned out that you had a very good eye for people who later became successful!

HH: Yes. Some of the other architects I featured were Odile Decq, Liz Diller and Ricardo Scofidio, Peter Zumthor, Ben van Berkel and Kazuyo Sejima.

WM: I think you had a great deal of impact on that generation in helping and pushing them to succeed.

HH: Well, the list includes two Pritzker Prize winners, and in the case of Sejima, she is now the director of the biennale as well.

AL: Do you find it difficult to exhibit architecture? When we spoke with Aaron Betsky, for instance, he acknowledged the difficulty of ever doing so successfully.

HH: I have no difficulty showing architecture or art!

WM: How did you choose those architects that you featured in 1996? I mean, did you go around asking people 'Who are the young, interesting architects?'

HH: I was connected with all kinds of people at the time. I knew many of them personally.

AL: Were you trying just to represent your community and everyone you knew at the time? Can you tell us more about how you decided to select these particular architects?

HH: I made a selection, and then they were invited to show their work – *their* work. And not something centred only on a specific topic or even my own theme. It was very much about the topic of the architect as seismograph, and I was trying to show the seismographic element of the architect who is sensing the future. This was an important criterion.

AL: As director, you also organised the 'Radicals' retrospective, which highlighted radical experiences of urban architecture from the end of the 1950s up to the early 1970s. Did you give these architects much direction? Or did you simply give them a space in which they could do whatever they liked?

HH: At that time these architects had very little work, but they were all given their own proper space, and not just a kind of cubicle. We also had a show on Austrian radicals in the national pavilion, complementing the international one.

WM: One of the things you said about the biennale at the time was that architects should be resistant to the idea of being part of schools of thought or movements. Do you recall that?

HH: Well, I don't disagree with this. The tendency at the time, I think, was in a different direction.

AL: Francesco Dal Co and others have explained how little money they had to work with. Did you have the same experience?

> HH: I had the same experience, and I had even less money than Francesco Dal Co! (Or basically the same.) The problem, though I don't want to talk too much about my predecessors, was that the *Strada Novissima* was a very interesting beginning, but then for a long time nothing happened with the architecture biennale. I wanted to pursue different ideas about how to display things, for example, I was interested in technology and in what one could do with various kinds of media in an exhibition. But I didn't have enough money.

AL: What do you feel was being lost in those shows where it was just drawings that were displayed on the wall? What was the problem for you with that approach?

> HH: Well, we have all seen these biennales where you walk for several kilometres in front of drawings. I have nothing against drawings, but at the time these drawings were still in pencil, and there were very few renderings. And drawings are too complex, while I wanted to address a different public. Unlike the art biennale, the architecture biennale sometimes received very little attention and was considered

just for insiders. I didn't want this. My biennale was the first one that had a new audience.

AL: So what you are saying is that yours was really the first architecture biennale that registered the emergent technologies of the time, and the new communication tools that were being incorporated into everyday practice.

HH: Yes, of course. Technology was also presented as an art here. At the time, renderings in today's sense were very rare.

AL: And as a curator you wanted to show that process of virtualisation, the way in which renderings were becoming a crucial means of representing architecture to others?

HH: Not necessarily. It was not just a question of showing a good drawing or rendering, there were a lot of models, too. Whenever we could, we included big models. Dal Co's biennale, which had come a few years before mine, was rather two-dimensional. It had featured some beautiful drawings but almost no models. And I find a model to be very good not only for exhibitions, but also for dialogues with clients – be it the mayor, or whoever.

AL: You felt that a model was something the general public could understand?

HH: Yes. It's like with a musical score. Certain things in architecture, like drawings, are more for the initiated, but others, like models, are easier to understand. Models can be translated three-dimensionally from a drawing.

AL: Is there anything that you wish you had done differently, looking back on the exhibition?

HH: There's a lot of pressure – I mean just to set up an exhibition and to get it there by boat is a nightmare! And as I mentioned before, we didn't have very much money. Of course today, when one has more money, there is no excuse for a bad exhibition. Unfortunately, we could not use the Corderie in the exhibition either. Otherwise, we could have had something on urbanism. But the Corderie was closed, so the exhibition was actually very small. You know, they wanted me to direct a second time after Fuksas' exhibition in 2000, but it was too much work for me.

AL: In 1996 the architecture biennale was still quite young, and still struggling to assert its independence from the art biennale. Were you trying to keep them separate by focusing on more formal definitions of architecture?

HH: I actually think it's okay if you sometimes have architecture in the art biennale and vice-versa. In Venice, you already have this underlying duality: you have the national pavilions, and then also the general biennale. And just as you can have a dialogue between these two aspects of the same biennale, so you can have a dialogue between the architecture and the art biennales. But although they sometimes overlap it is right and important that they are in two different sections.

WM: Can I ask you a question about your participation, as an architect, in 1980 in the *Strada Novissima*? Do you remember any of the conversations you had with Paolo Portoghesi, or did he just say 'You have this much space, and you can design whatever you want'? Was there any kind of discussion? Because now the *Strada Novissima* is seen by some people as a kind of beginning of postmodernism, but I don't think of you as a postmodernist.

HH: Everybody else, including Frank Gehry, created flat facades. However my idea was to address the space of the Corderie and its columns. So in my presentation some of those columns were represented. I put a model of the Chicago Tribune Tower in between two columns, and I even added a hanging column with no support from below. There is a photograph of Petra where you can see a column hanging down with no base in this way.

AL: Did you arrive at an idea of what you wanted to do in conversation with Portoghesi, or were you acting more independently and on your own?

HH: No, I acted independently. Portoghesi simply invited me, and I said that I don't think it's such a good idea to just make facades. So I just made this as I saw it, and it was actually the most talked about one!

AL: Today, shows such as Portoghesi's *Strada Novissima* are of canonical importance. At the time, was it apparent that they would be of such historical interest, or was there a more casual and informal feel to it all? Or to put it another way: did you anticipate how important the Venice Biennale would be for architecture today?

HH: Yes and no. In my own case, I don't know exactly why I was selected in those former exhibitions, or if they knew what I had done, but I think the people who selected me knew that I would come up with something different.

AL: When you were working in Venice, did you feel like you had to acknowledge the historical weight and significance of the city in what you were doing?

HH: The biennale in Venice is certainly the most important biennale in the world: Venice has hundreds of years of history, and the biennale itself is more than a hundred years old. But there are important exhibitions in other places that, like Venice, also have a strong cultural and architectural heritage. And Venice itself also has several hundred years of being other things. Of course, it is a place for art and culture, but it was also once a place for war. Just think of the Arsenale, after all, which was a former naval warehouse.

Massimiliano Fuksas

Paris
Wednesday 19 May 2010

Massimiliano Fuksas directed 'Less Aesthetics, More Ethics', the seventh architecture exhibition at the Venice Biennale. The exhibition, on display from 18 June to 29 October 2000 in the Arsenale and the Giardini, explored ethical approaches to contemporary architecture, acknowledging that architecture is no longer simply an aesthetic practice.

Aaron Levy and William Menking: We are interested in the beginnings of the biennale in the 1970s, and how difficult it is to show architecture in Venice. Above all, we want to talk to you about your biennale and the thought that went into it.

Massimiliano Fuksas: It's interesting that mine was 20 years after Portoghesi's exhibition in 1980. Portoghesi was the first to use the Corderie dell'Arsenale. With my biennale, I too wanted to do something very strong, and I wanted to start with a response to the art biennale because I was completely, absolutely convinced that architecture was much more interesting than visual art. I know it's a bit pretentious to say, but I think that there have been two strong biennales – Portoghesi's in 1980 and mine in 2000. Both have changed

something. If you do a biennale, it has to change
something. And my first idea in this respect
concerned my title, 'Less Aesthetics, More
Ethics'. I then spent about a year preparing for
the biennale, based on my meetings with Bruno
Zevi, my friend Peter Cook and others. Bruno
Zevi was my professor, my teacher in school. I
was always very aggressive towards him, just as
he was aggressive towards me. He was a fantastic, crazy guy, which is something that you
cannot find now. He was my enemy, my friend,
my father and my professor. At one point Zevi
said, 'What are you going to be doing for the
next ten years?' I answered, 'I'll do projects,
participate in some competitions.' 'No', he
responded, 'I am sure you will do good projects,
you are a great architect. But tell me, what do
you want to do for the next ten years?' In this
situation, one begins to ask oneself, what is
my life about, what am I doing with it, what is
life itself? Is it a programme or project, an idea
or something more that animates oneself? It's
something more, and it's more than being an
architect. So this is something that Zevi taught
me, that in the end it is not enough to be an
architect – even if you are a very good architect!
I want architects to participate in this change,
in this work about the reality of globalisation.
Twelve years ago when I started to work on
the biennale it was not so evident that this was
where one had to start. So when Baratta asked

me to be the director of the biennale, I proposed the title 'Less Aesthetics, More Ethics'. It is not that I don't believe in aesthetics; on the contrary, I believe it's much more than beauty. Aesthetics is a feeling; in Italian one thinks of the word *sentire*. But in any event, today aesthetics is not enough. And I said to Baratta, let's use all the space of the biennale; for the first time, let's use it *all*. Today, one has to find a new way to transmit information, and by information, I don't mean lights or video. For the 300m of the Corderie dell'Arsenale in which the exhibition unfolds, information means the confrontation between architecture and the world. The exhibition addressed the problems of water shortages, deforestation, fire and earthquakes. We organised a way to simultaneously use 36 projectors. The idea was to enable the public to see migrations, war, the problems in Rwanda, disasters and tornadoes. I had three or four teams of individuals that I sent all over the world to do this.

WM: And you decided which cities?

MF: Oh yes. We chose all the scenarios, from shopping centres to the biggest cities in the world, from Cairo to Tokyo, Mexico City to São Paulo. We approached the exhibition as if it were a project, a building. There were many kinds of visuality and architecture in it, ranging from those of Holland to those of Africa. And remember that the exhibition was entirely composed of videos and cinematic projections.

AL: You have acknowledged how important Portoghesi's biennale of 1980 was to you, on account of its dramatic qualities as well as its clear statement. Was your project aspiring to be a new *Strada Novissima*, an update to that earlier 'main street'?

MF: I think the two exhibitions are not the same, but they are similar in the way in which we both wanted to fix time. It's crazy to try to fix time, but we wanted to do it anyway. One day, one hour, one minute, one second of our life is there in that moment, in that period of the exhibition.

WM: Your biennale was so different from those that came before. It seemed less formal, more engaged with urbanism in a way.

MF: Yes, we definitely focused on urbanism. At that time, more than 50 per cent of the world was living in cities. When I reflected on this reality I felt that we had to do something in the exhibition that would explore the way we will live in cities in the future. Our home is old, and by home I don't mean the United States or London or even Rome; I mean our sense of community. I don't know how, but we have to learn to live together.

WM: So for you the biennale was an opportunity to engage with the real world rather than get into internal architecture arguments?

MF: Yes, I want to go beyond the specificity of architecture. There is no language in architecture. The language of architecture is exactly the same language of the world. We can all speak in the same way. The very expression of 'Less Aesthetics, More Ethics', which came from Zevi, communicated this clearly. Today, as conflicts and crises are consuming the financial system, politics and society, I feel that this expression remains very relevant.

AL: Only your biennale, and perhaps Burdett's, have developed along this trajectory which looks beyond the internal logic of architecture to question where we, as a society, are heading and what our responsibilities might be. Is it the responsibility of the biennale to encourage this sort of thinking more often?

MF: I don't know, and I don't want to say '*the* biennale'. Honestly there are so many things and possibilities inside the biennale. In my case, it is worth noting that I also did an exhibition online. I discovered, 12 years ago now, that we could work with the internet and with email, and therefore metaphorically if not actually with all the people in the world. We also did a book that was based on the online competition we held for young people.

AL: So the internet was part of your curatorial strategy, but in 2000, at an early juncture in its development, when it was far less ubiquitous than it is now.

MF: Yes, we started to work on the exhibition and the online component in 1998, because we had two years to prepare. I decided at the very beginning that architecture should not be a specialised language. Then art and architecture can live together, and architecture, after all, is part of art. There are no conflicts between artist and architects because they are exactly the same thing.

AL: You inaugurated a few awards with your biennale. Can you talk about those?

MF: I gave awards to three people that I loved. One was Paolo Soleri. Nobody remembered him at the time. Everybody said, 'Paolo Soleri, who is this guy?' He was lost in Arizona, working on his utopia, and the idea that we can live in a different way.

WM: And he was, with regard to the theme of your show, also very urban, in that he was trying to create this kind of new utopian urbanism.

MF: Another award was given to my friend Renzo Piano. It was impossible not to give him an award, as he is a friend.

WM: One thing we are interested in as we explore the history of the biennale are the student protests against the Golden Lion awards in 1968. Were you one of these students?

MF: Yes, of course!

WM: And the students had said that there should be no more Golden Lions?

MF: Yes. We were fighting very hard against this, and bear in mind the situation in Italy in 1968 – if in Paris it was one month in May, in Italy it went on for 10 years. We fought for a long time.

AL: But by 2000 that resistance to the award economy was over, it was no longer the fight to fight?

MF: Well, I didn't want to be in the jury over the awards. I only wanted to give awards to these guys that I admire.

WM: What do you think about some of the biennales that came after you?

MF: I cannot criticise them. Ricky Burdett tried to do something different. I think it was really interesting but not very spectacular. Think of the film festival at Cannes: if you show something you have to do something spectacular, otherwise it's boring. His team, his organisation, was perfect as a concept, but it was an exhibition. And when you show something like this, it has to be spectacular.

AL: In a certain sense, did you feel that Burdett's show was a sort of continuation of yours?

MF: Yes, I think that it was a part of my project. But I also think that Portoghesi, myself and Burdett are a sort of appendix to the biennale. I feel like an appendix. I think that was something that we did, to not show a building.

AL: What of Gregotti and his Molino Stucky? Did you feel that your exhibition was also attempting to address the future of Venice and questions such as the role that tourism would play in its future?

MF: But I think that the biennale starts with Portoghesi. His biennale took place in the Corderie dell'Arsenale. If you don't touch the Arsenale, it's not a biennale.

WM: When we talked to the architect and educator Massimo Scolari the other day, he remarked that you can't understand the biennales, particularly in the 1960s, without understanding the triennales.

MF: I think that if you stage a confrontation between Milan and Venice, Venice is much more international and Milan is really provincial.

WM: Provincial in terms of architecture?

MF: The city of Milan is very small, perhaps 800,000 or 900,000 people. Venice is an international city, and a really big one. You have well over 12 million people walking through the space of the city every year. It's crazy.

AL: Do you think of your exhibition as a project in itself, and list it alongside buildings you have designed in publications about your work?

MF: I wanted to introduce that way of thinking because an exhibition, a biennale, is an artwork. Our biennale was not an act of sociology, though. It was based on a feeling that the artist can confront the state of the world, can address the global situation, but it was much more about intuition than reality, because we are talking about the biennale, and the biennale is for the future, not for the past.

AL: Do you have regrets about what you did? Is there something you wish you could have done differently? Do you feel that there was a certain aspiration to build a sense of community that you didn't succeed in realising?

MF: I feel that there is no community of artists as there was between the nineteenth century and the twentieth century. There is a reason why there is no more avant-garde. I think the kind of biennale that I attempted can generate a new community of people. And my biennale was successful in that regard because it was something new; it was also unsuccessful, however, because it was not a winning system. Today you cannot have an avant-garde because every idea, every utopia, can be built in 20 minutes. In these circumstances the idea is no longer possible. What is utopia, and what is an avant-garde? To have whatever you want, to fly all over the world? This is not what the avant-garde is about. The star system that we have today is another world. Because we all build so fast we are no longer part of the avant-garde. Likewise, painting is done for when artists sell their works for millions. My biennale was the last temptation towards an avant-garde. I remember that Bruno Zevi had said to me, 'Please do a manifesto.' And I had said to him, 'No, I don't do that.'

AL: What did he want the manifesto to be?

MF: A 'Venice manifesto' about contemporary architecture and about revolutionary architecture. But this was the concept of a guy from another century, and it was not possible for me to do this.

AL: With your biennale, would you say that two stories unfolded, one in the public view and another behind the scenes? This second story would be the story of its production, involving money, politics, compromise and the like?

MF: I very much enjoyed working on the production of my biennale, because you cannot do a second biennale in your life. But no, I was fighting very hard against this development. Do you know why? I didn't want to be integrated. But when you are close to power these things happen. Without being conscious of it at all, you start to belong much more to power than you realise or want.

AL: How do you think we should place Aldo Rossi in our book of biennale conversations? Insofar as he is no longer alive, he is the only one we cannot interview. Perhaps just a photograph of the Teatro del Mundo? What do you think?

MF: I think that this was the best building

that he ever did. It is one of the most fantastic buildings! I was inspired by him during our biennale and I took the images of architects and projected them onto the facades of the city at night, along the Grand Canal. For one night only though, because on the second night, the police arrived and said you cannot do this.

AL: So, you were like a guerilla director to your own biennale?

MF: Yes. And it was a pleasure to do this.

AL: But this is also what the biennale is to you. It's not just what happened in the Corderie, it's also all of these gestures and experiments.

MF: It's like a happening, a continuous happening, an experiment.

AL: For the generation that comes after mine, who won't have had the chance to see your biennale in person, what would you like them to know about it? How would you communicate your biennale to them?

MF: I think I would say that it is not enough to be an architect. We have to give something more. An artist – a good artist – not an architect only, has to give. I feel that my project in Jaffa for Shimon Peres was really successful. I think

that with this project, which is about the search for peace, my mission was accomplished.
This was inside my biennale, at the end of the Arsenale.

AL: Does your catalogue accurately document and communicate what you did?

MF: I think that the catalogues of the biennale are not useful. This conversation that we are having right now is much more useful. The best biennale is the opening, and the day after, you can close. Like all exhibitions, you do it for one day, for one night, and afterwards you should close everything. It's just as good.

WM: Do you think there's still a reason to have architecture exhibitions, or does the internet make them less relevant?

MF: There are no reasons at all to have exhibitions of architecture. Even art exhibitions, because there are now different ways for artists to produce and communicate.

WM: But even today all the young architects really want to be in the Venice Biennale. It's so important to them! And maybe it's just because of what Venice is, its history.

MF: Well, everybody meets everybody. It's not

that people meet in architecture, as Sejima
is arguing, but rather that architects meet in
architecture. It's simply a big festival.

WM: People still go and love to be there.

MF: Why not? There are many people, many
things that are more dangerous than a biennale.
So we can keep the biennales. But I think the
biennale is the memory of the last century, the
beginning of the last century. Remember that
the biennale is over 100 years old. Do we really
think today that each young guy is showing
something interesting? No. But we will
continue to do it, because we are very romantic.
The world is very romantic.

Deyan Sudjic

London
Friday 21 May 2010

Deyan Sudjic directed 'Next', the eighth architecture exhibition at the Venice Biennale. The exhibition, on display from 8 September to 3 November 2002 in the Arsenale and the Giardini, explored future architecture, with a particular concentration on new developments in urban and skyscraper design.

Aaron Levy and William Menking: We would like to focus specifically on your biennale, 'Next'. How did you conceptualise it in terms of the history of the biennale – in relation to what came before and where architecture was at that particular moment?

Dejan Sudjic: I was very struck, I suppose, by what was going on in 2002. There had never been more work for architects: there was no one who couldn't build if they wanted to, so there was no avant-garde. The future was always being built, and it seemed futile to invite busy architects to talk about their work and make installations with limited budgets because they weren't going to do anything of any interest compared to what they were actually building. And I also felt uncomfortable with the way previous directors had curated the biennale.

93

AL: So how did you arrive then at what was shown? How did you conceptualise what form it would ultimately take?

DS: I suppose what I did was very Anglo-Saxon. It was a pragmatic, very conservative and very traditional exhibition in that it showed physicality. I was inspired, to some extent, by an exhibition that Herzog & de Meuron had done the summer before – a very elegant collection of process models, juxtaposed with some fantastic full-sized material mockups, including a piece of wall in their Tokyo Prada shop. It was just so beautiful, and the Prada piece was not unlike the Corderie in that it's a found space. So that really got me going, in the sense of thinking about how you could collect work from around the world that showed how the world was going to be. It was a very simple, almost banal idea.

WM: So you had a year?

DS: Well, eight months. I was appointed as a director in December the previous year. In a way, the less time you have the better because you don't speculate too much. Anyway, the title came to me in a conversation with the biennale's president, Paolo Baratta, in Rome. And from that conversation, in July, it took another four months to get the appointment before the board. Then very soon afterwards, Baratta was fired. In spite of these developments, I wanted to produce an exhibition that was organised in a cohesive way rather than being a kind of free-for-all. So I did some very boring things with the exhibition design like insist on the same graphic style throughout, because so often in previous years it had looked to me like a kind of disorganised mess.

WM: It's hard for me to remember what it must have been like at the time, but Asia is very much at the centre of things now, and it seemed to be a major part of what you were already doing back then.

DS: It wasn't at the centre of things then. Harald Szeemann, the director of the previous biennale for art, had said to me that I should look at this project in Beijing, the Great Wall commune. This was in early 2002, at a time when China's architectural development was utterly invisible and the Chinese often had difficulty getting visas, and so we showed that in the exhibition. It was fascinating, because at the time no one had seen or heard anything about contemporary China.

AL: What about your section of the exhibition entitled 'City of Towers', related to the Twin Towers and September 11th?

DS: Well, the show was going to open exactly a year after 9/11 and it seemed like a good idea to commission something – not on such a large scale as Portoghesi's *Strada Novissima*, but nevertheless a gesture for people to think about: Is the large tower dead? It was an exploration of visceral feeling that I had while I was sitting in my office at Domus, watching the 9/11 towers come down. I asked six people to do a tower, and Alessi ended up supporting it. The towers that we had specially designed and fabricated for the exhibition were enormous – the size of the room itself. Future Systems did one, Zaha Hadid did one, Morphosis did one, Chipperfield too, and others. It was a fascinating project, trying to get it all to fit in the Corderie. They were 1:100 scale, so they were very tall, and literally reached into the rafters!

AL: So that's what you meant when you were saying that, in a certain sense, you were referencing Portoghesi?

DS: Yes, I wanted something big, made especially for the biennale. For me, the experience of negotiating the Arsenale is exhausting. It's hot and it's a mess, and you need to vary the pace to get people through it all. So the idea was to begin with these quite tidy and tightly organised thematic bits, then suddenly have a pause with the towers, before you turn the corner and go back to the thematics.

AL: And by thematic bits, you mean that there were sections on housing, on museums, on education, on church and state, on shopping among others. Could you talk a bit more about that taxonomic approach? Was this classificatory regime something that you felt was important, or that had been missing in past years?

DS: It was just a way to organise it, in the most banal and unambitious way.

WM: How did the press respond to your desire to return to a more formal engagement with architecture and the language of architecture?

DS: Well, I think in Britain it was seen as being elegant, a powerful affirmation of a particular moment in architecture. But some of the Italians, who are seduced by rhetoric, felt that this was, well, they used the word 'conservative' so many times! But there were so many things going on during the biennale. The American pavilion was full of photographs of 9/11 by Joel Meyerowitz. I remember Joel rang me up one day and said, 'You know, I've got a piece of twisted steel from Ground Zero.' And we actually had a conversation about reconstructing 9/11. Herbert Muschamp had commissioned this project of rebuilding Ground Zero in *The New York Times*. And we brought all those photographs over and installed them and had a conversation about them, which was interesting.

AL: Looking back on the history of the US pavilion, that was a year in which a commercial magazine, *Architectural Record*, was functioning as a commissioning organisation, and a commercial gallery, Max Protech, was also involved. Did that seem problematic at the time to you?

DS: Compared to the Italians, who had their own forms of sponsorship, why should it? No, it's not a problem. At the art biennales all those installations depend on dealers paying for the pieces. How do you think that Richard Serra managed to make an installation there?

WM: Was Venice a difficult place in which to work?

DS: No, I loved it, and who wouldn't love working in Venice? I do remember Renzo Piano saying, when I called him to talk about what project he might come up with, 'You know of course I'd love to, but be careful with the people of the Lagoon. On the surface they're very friendly, but under the water they want to bite your legs!' Now I never found this to be the case! It was a really good time working there.

WM: So Baratta hired you, and then he was essentially fired just as you arrived? [He has since been reappointed.]

DS: I described Baratta in a piece I wrote for *The Guardian* as having the amused gravitas of someone who could play a Cardinal in the remake of *The Godfather*. Baratta has been very important in expanding the biennale out of the Giardini and into the Arsenale, where it has taken more space over from the navy and renovated it. He has put the whole institution on some kind of sensible commercial footing. I mean, he has used the biennale for the cultural and physical regeneration of Venice in a very important way. He's also an effective politician.

AL: We loved working in Venice, but we also to this day remember how impossible it was. Are there things that you regret not being able to do?

DS: Yes, the fireworks! There was a budget for fireworks for the opening night, and there was some nonsense about the heritage lobby taking six months to give the go-ahead, after you'd proved that your fireworks weren't going to damage the city fabric. As to other regrets, well I wish that they'd paid the bill for Zumthor to transport his models back. He had this gigantic concrete model of the Cologne museum, and for three months I was determined to get it to

Venice. Dragging this thing down the Alps, putting it on a barge, shipping it across the lagoon... What's that film with Klaus Kinsky in which he drags the steamboat across the hill in the Amazon?

AL: You mean Werner Herzog's film *Fitzcarraldo*?

DS: I felt like that. It was just fantastic. But once the stuff got to Venice, the budget suddenly shifted.

AL: It's interesting to hear you talk about the show, and also to hear you talk about Venice, which was the context for all this. Could you talk a little more about Venice as a city? It has developed even further as a tourist destination since the year you organised your biennale. Were you thinking about this as you were doing 'Next'?

DS: Well, of course you respond physically to the context. The time I spent there made me feel differently about Venice. The sense of being there at night, the daily walk from the director's apartment to the site – you begin to engage with all this in a different way, for a moment you feel as if you are taken into this world. The idea of being locked into Harry's Bar after closing time, and taking the *vaporetto* home with people you began to recognise, that was great. But I was trying to make an exhibition addressed to those who were not part of the architectural priesthood. And we had the best visitor numbers for a biennale at that stage because it made sense to a normal specialist, I suppose. Obviously, before the opening weekend Venice is transformed, and for that moment the world of architecture is focused on that one place.

AL: Being a working critic and journalist, how did that influence what you did and how you presented it?

DS: I remember actually talking to Baratta about this. You wouldn't actually have a working artist curating the art biennale, for the sake of objectivity, but of course I wasn't really developing a thesis, except that I was interested in materiality, and in looking at the astonishing effort that actually goes into a building as opposed to an installation. I suppose that as a working critic I may have had the vanity to want to put a few more words in. I had been travelling a lot at the time, and that means you start to see the world in a way that nobody else does. I mean how many people will actually go to Seattle to see the main library, say, and then off to Milan or wherever? I suppose you consume all these links today in a ridiculously rapid way. I mean, I spend half an hour in a building and believe I've got it.

AL: So how did you reconcile your predilection for language with the sheer heterogeneity of the public? Your audience doesn't all speak the same language, and you have such a short time in which to engage them in the first place.

DS: For the catalogue I commissioned a series of essays about major themes, such as shopping. In the case of the exhibition, you keep it short. At the entry to the exhibition, I tried to make a series of points on the wall based on actual things that were going to happen: here is a place, and if you come here, you will see the world of architecture as it will be in five years' time.

WM: So much of what 'Next' was about was the future. In retrospect, how much of it do you think you got right?

DS: Well, some people were not actually going to get these things built, of course. But I think it all reflected a very particular moment, when there was no longer any avant-garde, because the avant-garde was building like crazy.

AL: I have a somewhat different question: what's the difference between architecture and design today? Do you curate them both in the same way? Are they becoming the same thing?

DS: Well, it's a particularly Italian question. They had been regularly talking about having a design biennale in Venice, so you start to wrestle with what you would do. The scale is different in the case of design. Also you are thinking about a different set of issues, including customisation, the dematerialisation of objects and other things. *Domus* is one of those magazines that is embracing design, art and architecture as part of the same conversation, which doesn't happen that often.

AL: One of the things that Portoghesi had attempted to do was to leave something behind through this renovated Arsenale. Did you have the aspiration to leave something physical behind, or was that not the point of your biennale?

DS: You can't do everything. I spent four years in Glasgow working on a series of cultural events there. And that was about leaving things behind. In Venice you know you're making a spectacle, and you want to make it as beautiful as you can.

AL: Did you have a history with the biennale before your selection?

DS: Apart from going there personally, no. I was the editor of *Domus*, however, which was the kind of constituency that Baratta was looking to at the time for input into how the biennale was being regarded.

AL: Speaking from our own experience, working at the biennale was a highpoint of our recent practice. Did you feel the same toward your biennale? Was it a transformative experience or moment for you?

DS: It was a fantastic thing to do. It was my 50th birthday on the day the show opened. My mother died that year and I also got married in Venice. It was a very personal and extraordinary year. But it's good not to repeat yourself in life. And it's been very useful to what I've done here. To measure yourself against that kind of audience, to wrestle with the egos that are involved? It gives you the kind of skills you need to do it again and, certainly, it transformed my life.

Kurt W Forster

New York
Friday 26 February 2010

*Kurt W Forster directed 'Metamorph', the ninth
architecture exhibition at the Venice Biennale.
The exhibition, on display from 12 September to
7 November 2004 in the Arsenale and Giardini,
explored how new technologies and materials have
directed the metamorphosis of architecture.*

Aaron Levy and William Menking: We're
interested in 'Metamorph', your exhibition for the
2004 biennale, and whether your thoughts about
it have developed and changed in the years since
it closed. But we also have some questions for
you concerning your work as a curator. We're particularly interested in how a sense of spectacle and
touristic expectations in a city such as Venice
are impacting the practice of architectural display
and curation. We're also interested in the degree
to which one has to acknowledge today the rich
history that always precedes one's own gestures.
I suppose our first question is a historical one: how
did the history of the biennale affect what you did
with your biennale?

Kurt W Forster: That's a very interesting
subject. I came to the biennale at a moment

when there were massive changes, not only
in its administration but also in its own self-
understanding and its public role. Franco
Bernabè, who was the president at that
moment, is a very classy financier at the highest
international levels. He was not only versed in
international dealings of every kind, but was
also an independently wealthy man who took
that favourable condition as a launch pad to
attempt something that went beyond the usual
limits. I think the very fact that he asked me to
take this on is, if anything, a testimony to the
way he took the broadest possible international
view of this biennale. He didn't put any faith in
the questions that one always has to deal with
in Italy, and strove to go beyond the national
horizon. The first question any Italian journalist
is always going to ask is, how many Italians are
in your biennale? The biennale, in the view
of the Italians, ought to be an Italian biennale,
but on the other hand they know perfectly
well that it can't be. And they try to negotiate
between the necessity of having the biennale
address the world and bringing the world to
Venice, and the fact that everything in Venice
is supposed to be Venetian and everything in
Italian. They negotiate this discrepancy by
trying to put numbers on you and to weigh and
evaluate you. I had actually many more Italians
than either my predecessor or successors, but
I put them all where they belong, in what was

called *Notizie dall' interno*, the 'News from Inside the Country', which Mirko Zardini curated. We did it together, but he was the man ultimately responsible for that section. I did that deliberately, so as to not offend anybody, because I had been living in Italy long enough to know that I shouldn't set out to offend, because whatever I did I would end up doing so anyway. At that moment when everyone was asking how much it was all going to cost I felt authorised, with Bernabè in charge, to go ahead in a way that would probably have been difficult for my predecessors. Unfortunately, the general political administrative climate was too ungainly and too tiresome for Bernabè to continue to deal with, and so he left. Literally from one day to the next.

AL: In the middle of your preparations?

KF: Well, I was only a couple of months into the work, which is typically assigned to you in ungodly haste. It's always late, and one has come to understand what that means. Then there was a hiatus of several months, where the biennale was in receivership, so to speak. And then they finally arrived at the choice of Davide Croff as the new president. And from that moment on, the entire climate changed. Everything was merely a question of could you operate within the budget, were you on schedule? And of course it's very hard to tell someone you're on schedule if there's nothing to see around you! Only when the crates actually arrive can you be sure that the work has been done. So most of the preparation for the biennale was done under the incredibly encouraging and enthusiastic Bernabè, but then all of it had to be realised, down to the most painful pulling of teeth, under another kind of administration. I'll give you only one example, which I'm proud to remind anybody of. We were in the very last days of mounting everything. I had obtained from Frank Gehry a loan of all the study models for the Bilbao Guggenheim, and his office had finished the panels that would give all the construction documents and details – they were of great interest at that moment because everyone was mystified by the construction aspect of that building. Then the principal financial administrator of the biennale came to my office and said 'We don't have any money, we can't print them!' So I paid for them to be printed. We were lucky that we could sell them afterwards, to a Gehry fan in Rome, so I actually came out of it without serious damage. But it was several thousand euros, as you can imagine. So in terms of the administrative 'support', I think that's the best illustration of what we had to deal with.

AL: It's interesting that you begin with this

description of the administrative and logistical complexity, because this was not only our experience, but something that Francesco Dal Co and others have told us is a perennial problem. This raises the question: to what degree is curating today determined by these aspects?

KF: *There*, at the biennale, it is. But it's a virulent issue in many places. It hits everybody: whether you're prepared for your job, whether you know how to do it, whether you deliver on time and on budget or not – it really makes no difference. The budget and scheduling are held over your head as a kind of cudgel.

WM: You were in this awkward situation where they wanted to expand the reputation and impact of the biennale, but with no financial support.

KF: None, and at the same time they almost doubled the surface that was put at my disposal. So you had a serious issue of stagecraft and stage management, if you will. On the other hand, all this becomes negligible because of the fantastic opportunity that these locations provide. I spent an incredible amount of time working with the individual representatives of all the countries and with the designers and installers to ensure there was enough gravity to the overall theme, so that it would begin to pull what they were doing into orbit. But I must say

I was very happy to do it, and I think it produced interesting results.

AL: Did you find yourself reluctantly accepting these entanglements, or did you enjoy the intensity of it, the compromises it forced you to confront?

KF: No, I've done many things which have strong political dimensions and complications, you know. I was the founding director of the Getty Research Institute, I directed the Canadian Centre for Architecture for a number of years, and I ran the Architecture History and Criticism Department of the ETH in Zurich, which is a public school in every sense – you negotiate with government representatives over almost every paper clip.

WM: In Venice, were you ever given a budget?

KF: The curious thing is that the budget is a kind of elaborate conspiracy, because many things have to be paid out of the money that comes to the biennale as an institution. Don't forget that at my time there were five different biennales on various topics in the arts, and only the president and his trusted co-conspirators knew where the money was for these and how it could be used. So at any one moment they could tell you you were over your budget on mineral water!

AL: When you used the word 'stagecraft' it reminded me of something Paolo Baratta said, which is that a good director, as well as the work of the institution itself, is very much caught up in stagecraft. It also recalls Portoghesi's *Strada Novissima* exhibition of 1980, and how that was very much centred on a theatrical kind of model of display.

KF: I think that's a very important point. Of course the biennale has to be staged. After all, you solicit the interest and the arrival of all of this public, and then what do they see? They're not going to look at pictures on a wall. Portoghesi's *Strada Novissima* wanted to project the idea that architecture is made of very many strands and textures. And I tried to respond to that, almost a quarter of a century later, by making it appear when you entered into the long gallery that a kind of flotilla of proposals was coming to the harbour. So you could look down over this space, and through it, and you would have all of these things almost miraculously arrive towards you.

WM: Were the asymptotes and plinths meant to be gondolas?

KF: But it was mercifully unnaturalistic! What we wanted was that you would get this sense that you were *not* walking into a box, not going to go from one chamber to another, but that you would actually see the world come floating towards you. In that moment in architecture, at the beginning of the new millennium, I think people wanted something like that. You wanted to get this impression that you were looking out over an ocean of possibilities.

AL: The *Strada Novissima* was in a sense about popularising architecture and trying to engage not just with a specialised discourse but with the general public as well. Did you feel that your show was doing something different? To be slightly reductive, to whom was it addressed?

KF: I didn't have in mind a public that was more specialised or more prepared than before. What I felt was important was to point out some directions and to suggest the new alliances architecture was making with vast, complex organisations. We looked at the 'hyperstructures' that were being constructed on river embankments in Lyon, Paris, London – vast complexes embracing everything from public transportation, open park sites, museums, conference centres, residencies and hotels. You had this kind of ball of wax that suddenly was able to absorb previously incompatible ingredients, a new kind of hybrid, interrelated architecture, which was certainly a very important trend. Another one was to say that some architecture doesn't just simply lend itself to representation in images but that on every level, in every detail, there is a genuine affinity between architecture and images. That is why we brought in all that photography. All of a sudden you saw that photographers are looking at mountains not to see the sunset, but to see all the hidden entry doors for trucks during wartime, or looking at the Great Wall of China not as a tourist trap, but in relation to previous Walls of China that are now just dusty furrows in the landscape. We brought all this in to encourage reflection, refraction. The idea was great: you came into the Arsenale and you had this three-screen arrangement.

WM: That was the first thing you saw?

KF: It was the first thing you saw. The natural and the mechanical were opposed, showing how a familiar territory could be re-used and looked at through a new lens, with new interests and new possibilities.

WM: It's exactly what Aaron Betsky did in his later biennale, no? On entering the Arsenale the first image you encountered was a visual one, concerning the history of architecture and film.

KF: Yes, I believe so, but it's not something that you come up with as a kind of invention.

In those years, the terrain was already shifting and you could no longer split architecture off from its media presence. You had to bring them together somehow. That's why the very first thing you came to in the Corderie was this kind of farewell to four architects who were all dead, and who had previously defined architecture in a particular way.

AL: Did you articulate this move in relation to prior exhibition models? Was it singular to your project?

KF: I thought it was representative of the condition of architecture. I was trying to propose that people should entertain the thought that architecture itself was changing, becoming a new species. That's why we called it 'Metamorph'. It is now moving, as it were, out of the water and becoming a reptile. It is acquiring all sorts of potential that it didn't have before, and it can't operate in the same way that earlier exhibitions had envisioned it as operating. And I think that was simply feeling the pulse of the moment, which is necessary for an exhibition of that kind. With other kinds of architecture exhibitions, the dilemmas are different. To make an architecture exhibition is often an exercise in either futility or redundancy. You show the plans and photographs again and again. You bring in architectural models to illuminate the process of working. But I think exhibitions where you bring in truckloads of your working archive become a little bit of a cliché. With 'Metamorph', we tried, in a sense, to follow the metabolism of ideas and how they finally arrive at a building. Because that's the other question, which is that one doesn't know anymore how you arrive at the actual building.

WM: Right. And you tried to show that?

KF: We tried in some instances to show it.

WM: As in the case of Gehry?

KF: Exactly. But you illustrate it all in a very selective way, obviously. Because a story told in too much detail often becomes impenetrable. The more documentation you provide, the more complicated and unresolvable the case becomes.

AL: The more documentation you provide, the less transparent and legible it becomes for the public.

KF: Right. You provide it for that purpose, but you're defeated by your own strategy. Frank Gehry approached it very didactically: here is the shoebox model, and here is Disney Concert Hall. How do you get from one to the other? You get to this in a kind of classic fashion by appropriating something. Frank thought of it as a baseball glove, as a mitt. In other words, he wanted to hold music, as it were, in his hands. Therefore all of these things can begin to move. But the hand is fundamentally symmetrical. And of course the amazing thing is that the Disney Hall is completely symmetrical, in the end, but you come to it by all of these exertions.

AL: So you would say that it's not just the building that represents architecture, but the process?

KF: I think in the end, process becomes architecture for the simple reason that you're not just sitting in your chair and looking at a laptop. The point of the exhibition is to gain some real sense of what this architecture that you're exhibiting is about.

AL: But how exactly did you do that in Venice?

KF: Well, that was almost not possible in Venice. The only way I could do it was to invite architects to build a kind of 'episode' room. The same builders who were at that time building the Mercedes Museum by Ben van Berkel constructed one incredible, full-scale double curve of a segment while the biennale was going on. That was an attempt to literally lift, or transport a piece of a building, however fragmentary, from its original site to the site of the exhibition. In the main hall of the Italian section, we had elastic nets and fabric with objects from daily life, ranging from the rural to the urban, from the modern to the ethnographic. And there was a frieze of photographs that captured modern situations. You had in a sense two forms of archive: you had a narrative archive that captured something from real life, and you had the forensic archives – found weapons, traces left behind, the fragments that survive. Similarly, as you came from the embankment, what Hani Rashid decided to do was to begin almost imperceptibly with a form like a bench going in, which then becomes a funnel opening up. And from that moment on you were on a sort of curving trajectory. We completely remapped the progress through the Italian pavilion. And I had a hyperbaric chamber where Peter Eisenman compressed 500 years of architecture from Palladio to his latest building in Santiago, as deformations of their own elements. It was very much in the spirit of the show that you could actually see the metamorphosis – you could see something that was a straight pipe here, and then all of a sudden it began to twist, as if the centuries were exerting their own weight and power on things.

WM: You literally reoriented how people went through the Italian pavilion?

KF: Yes. This pavilion is of course impossible, it's like a block of cheese, to which new wedges have been added again and again. There is still the old octagon, which is the only part that remains; then there is the fascist front that has been added; and from behind, up to the canal, new volumes have also been glued to it. So what we did is perform a kind of double under and over and out again. And that was possible because in most places there were only sheetrock partitions, and we just cut openings into those. We got the agreement of the administration because we could easily put it back, and it was carefully planned so that you would always be 48m from a fire exit. What you got were very interesting views through and across the space. You got a sense of somebody gesturing at the scale of the space. You could look through and see all these traces in the sand of Kengo Kuma's robot, and at the end the silvery shell of the Disney Concert Hall. When you talk about staging an exhibition, the important thing is to keep in mind that the visitor is not in an armchair, and there are always dimensions that can be tapped, opened up.

AL: But you were not just reframing or transforming the interior landscape, you were also attempting to change the external landscape of the Giardini.

KF: Yes. Actually, I wanted to do much more,

and I have wonderful documentation on that made by Emilio Trabella, who is one of the principal horticulturists in Italy. Together we documented the state of the vegetation in the biennale grounds, and the diagnosis was devastating. Half the trees were mortally ill, and one actually fell down and smashed a bench. I said to Davide Croff, look, you've got to do something about these trees, because one day they're going to come down. They're falling down entirely because they're rotting, and they have been cut very badly. Nobody had done anything, because it's the garbage department that is in charge.

AL: But isn't that organic atmosphere of the Giardini so crucial to the identity of the biennale?

KF: Yes, of course. Now my plan was to do something with the Giardini, because no one ever does anything about it. They put in a little more gravel, and they occasionally lop off falling branches. I proposed to 'metamorph' the gardens by initiating a campaign to recover them as a horticultural project. It would obviously be very limited in scale, given the short duration of the biennale, but wherever you went you would see something of it. You would see, for instance, certain trees cut in a completely different way, and new trees planted. You would see those silly hedges had been removed. I was thinking of how the Japanese have always done things under their pavilion because it is on stilts, and so forth. In 2003 Sejima, I think, put all these white little artificial marguerite flowers underneath it and wrapped the pavilion in white. So I proposed it to Davide Croff, and he of course fought me. I went off to meet the head of public sanitation. And this guy didn't understand a word of what I was saying. He simply couldn't conceive – this had never happened in his life-time, in his profession – that somebody would come and talk about the garden in terms other than the masses of leaves that have to be removed when they fall, or the branches that have to be chipped up, or cut off. He simply could not understand and he said I was making fun of him. And I said, well, the fun will start when the first tree will fall. And just a couple of weeks later a tree came down. It crashed down, and they never repaired it. They didn't have the money to repair it, probably.

AL: They should have left the tree there as a sort of decaying monument to what the Giardini had become.

KF: They should have. But it would have been a public obstacle. Anyway, there will be more falling trees; take my word for it.

AL: It's interesting that you bring this up. When

120

we talked to Francesco Dal Co, and Portoghesi too, we learned a great deal about how they had seen their biennale not just as a project of display but also one of restoration, of rehabilitation. In a way, you were proposing something similar.

KF: Yes. All of these great, and in a sense logical, plans of using the occasion in order to kick-start neglected things, to initiate at least a symbolic campaign so that people say, well now it looks much better, maybe we should finish it – all that is perceived as completely utopian.

AL: Everything that would change or deviate from the tradition becomes utopian?

KF: Basically, you have to understand that in Venice, there is a natural tendency to cling to things the way they are, but that tendency is becoming hysterical. In Venice, nobody does you the favour. We are now below 50,000 permanent residents – can you imagine, as a tax base and so forth? But we're expecting four million more visitors. So the entire town has become purely a theatre. The people who are still living there, if they're not students, are involved in maintaining this theatre. Apart from the students, there is nobody living in Venice who is not engaged in either maintaining or servicing it as a tourist destination.

AL: Did you feel that tension then? We clearly felt it in working on our exhibition.

KF: Yes, it doesn't ever go away.

AL: And did you feel you can't compete with it, on a certain level?

KF: No, I think you have to ride it, so to speak. This is not only a trend, it's like the sea level!

AL: Yes, but at the end of the day one has to come to terms with the realities of exhibition-making. And there's this brutal realisation that creeps in that an exhibition can only do so much.

KF. But I think you can seek different terms. Your accommodation can also leave certain things visible, so that they become the object of attention. And I think I did this with the gardens. I'm not sure how far it will go, but this is not so important in and of itself. I think I made people realise that there's something wrong with this garden, by making hints, pointing to certain possibilities. You need only to inject one element to change the perception of a far larger area.

AL: When I think back to your past positions and institutional affiliations, I notice a clear pedagogical and discursive trajectory. Your time at the Getty and the Canadian Centre for Architecture, for instance, is marked by that legacy. But in your biennale, it seems like that interest of yours in the pedagogical just wasn't there.

KF: That's one of my defeats, I have to admit. You can only do certain things, and I think I wanted very much to do more by bringing in architecture schools.

WM: What do you think of other biennales that have tried to deal with contemporary issues in the way that Burdett, for instance, tried to do in focusing on questions of density and urban conditions?

KF: I was involved with Aaron Betsky in a couple of interesting debates. It is very difficult in a situation like ours, where everybody is used to forcefully structured propositions, to a kind of honed discourse that has a thrust, an orientation, a purpose and a character. It is very difficult in this moment to go back to images, graphs, schemes and statistics on a wall. You can look at 10 maps of London, and you can see anything. You're thrown back to a kind of attention and response that is now in the domain of technical discourse. So it's almost impossible to make an exhibition out of that. And the question is: is an exhibition an effective platform to bring out these problems?

AL: For a brief moment each year Venice seems to be centre-stage, but after the buzz recedes it's often very hard to figure out what happened. You can't just deduce it from the catalogue, as the catalogue is often printed beforehand. And the internet is fairly unreliable as well.

KF: I changed the whole catalogue business because I thought it was cumbersome, unnecessary and sort of gratuitous. What actually is the relationship of this huge awkward thing to the exhibition? Why should anybody lug around 700g of essays that they're not going to read anyway? They're not expected to, so I split them off. And we also tried to do it in the design by using indexing and colours, to make it more like a manual.

AL: One of the things that Baratta explained to us was the sheer complexity of trying to archive the biennale. He communicated the struggle over how to document not just the first biennales but also the more recent ones, which have invariably played out over BlackBerrys and email trails.

KF: Well it's a much bigger problem than that of the BlackBerry. If the biennale had preserved its own papers systematically and in responsible fashion, you would have had a singular body of evidence on which you could write dissertations for the next decade. The terrible thing is that the biennale has been a little bit like the presidential libraries, in that it has been raided periodically by various figures who made off with parts of it. The point is, it's like one of those banks in Liechtenstein. It has an address and a director, but nobody knows what's there and nobody can ever access it.

AL: Would you say that you were left to yourself, in a way, to figure out what the history of the biennale was for architecture?

KF: Yes. I think the need for uncovering this history is the reason behind Baratta's initiative to bring all the directors back to Venice during Sejima's biennale. He's trying to tap into the history, and I think it's a great idea. And I know there is a lot of interest in this, because one always looks through the biennale as if it were a magnifying glass.

AL: Are you interested today in revisiting your exhibition to explore how these questions and ideas could be better framed with the benefit of hindsight? Or are you not interested in looking back at this time?

KF: I feel that it would be much more interesting, in my case, to have a further conversation with the people I involved. That might be a very interesting weekend. I believe a first step is

Baratta's attempt to bring in the directors and have them deal with the latest instalment of this. So the idea is kind of bifocal – you have your own biennale, from some time back, and now you've got the latest. And what does that do to your vision of things?

WM: But he's not going to bring them all at one time.

KF: No, we will come as part of a series. I think he probably fears for the public if he brought us all at one time!

Richard Burdett

London
Monday 17 May 2010

Richard Burdett directed 'Cities: Architecture and Society', the tenth architecture exhibition at the Venice Biennale. The exhibition, on display from 12 September to 7 November 2006 in the Arsenale and the Giardini, explored issues of density, mobility and sustainability in global cities such as Mumbai, Tokyo and Bogotá.

Aaron Levy and William Menking: We are interested in the complicated origins and history of the biennale as an institution and in the way each director has altered its trajectory in organising their respective exhibitions. We are also interested in the complexity of showing architecture today. Could you talk about your show and how you defined the theme? Why did you decide to highlight urbanism and focus throughout on cities? Was that due to a perceived deficiency in past biennales?

Richard Burdett: In the summer of 2004 I was contacted by the then president of the biennale who said they had decided on the theme for the next biennale, which would look at the issue of cities. So in that sense it was a given. It wasn't 'Ricky, would you like to do this? Well choose what you want to do, look at the previous nine, and decide.' What I ended up doing was not a conscious critique of what had happened before; it was more an intellectual statement, given this theme that I was invited to look at. What is wonderful about this mad organisation that is the biennale is that it is run by a relatively small group of civil servants. One moment they are dealing with my exhibition about the streets of Caracas and crime, and the next they're dealing with Sejima's wonderful white spaces. It's the same with art, music and film. I'll tell you a little anecdote as an observation about the profound connection between the biennale and Italian politics – with all of its drawbacks and its advantages. I was asked at some point, probably in September 2004, to go in front of the board and to present my ideas. I didn't have one written document with me, neither an example nor a budget – for the whole cycle there was in fact no written exchange. So I'm invited to the board meeting and I don't know who's going to be there: no list of names was provided. I walk into this extraordinary room in a palazzo overlooking the Grand Canal and I see the biennale president Davide Croff, whom I have met before. He is a very successful businessman, but not particularly noted for his relationship to culture, and certainly not to architecture. Croff is in the middle, with two others to the left and two to the right of him.

I think this must be the board of directors of the five different disciplines – the one on the left is possibly art, the one on the extreme left is responsible for dance, and the one on the right is possibly film. But it becomes absolutely clear that the two to the left are a socialist and a radical ex-communist. They are on the left politically, and represent the city of Venice and other political contingencies. The ones to the right represent the right politically, advocating for the region and part of the government. So here I am, with cultural ideas that have to be blessed by a group of people who don't have a great connection to the subject. And it means one thing – that you're totally on your own. Being the director of the biennale is an extraordinary and terrifying experience. You realise that you have at your disposal something that will be visited by hundreds of thousands of people. Even if you do it wrong, they will come. And you're on your own for the infrastructure to deliver it, because there's no one there who is on the same intellectual page as you – otherwise why are they bringing you in? How do you take this very large rabbit out of a hat, and make something happen in an incredibly short period of time? I think Betsky had a very tough time with the programme he was given. If I were given five months, as he was, I would have done it too, because you don't say no to an opportunity like this. But I think this is something that's quite difficult to understand from outside. That being said, if you think back to Aldo Rossi's Teatro del Mundo, everything is possible: it's just a question of how you manage that process and how you play your politics. I do think that an outsider like myself is at a massive disadvantage. My situation is particularly amusing, though, because everyone in Italy, and everyone on the board, assumed that because my name is Richard Burdett that I have no Italian connections at all. When I asked them if I should speak in Italian or English, there was a serious sense of disappointment because I felt that they thought, well, if we'd known he was Italian then we could have had one of 'our' boys or girls direct! I bring this point forward because one has to understand how extraordinary this machine is, how fragile it is. The biennale is always afraid of spending too much money. But how fantastic it is that a government like Italy, which doesn't need to do this, especially in a time that's so difficult financially, makes the effort to do it. But it very quickly becomes an issue of developing an idea, then finding someone who can do it. And this is one of those things that probably shapes what you're doing more than any massively intellectual concept: the pragmatics of filling a 300m-long space. Having been given the framework, what I decided to do was totally connected to what information and material

I thought I could assemble in a reasonably short period of time that would look good and tell a narrative. And the narrative in my mind was very simple, very clean, and probably concerned with what I still do today: that there is a fundamental link, one that is not well understood, between the space we design and inhabit and social well-being – that is, a link between the physical world and the social world, which plays out more in cities than in buildings. You can have a badly designed hospital that works perfectly well if you have good doctors, whereas it's pretty difficult to have a horribly designed piece of modern housing that works for the residents who are there. So that was the overarching concept, and I thought: I have the biennale, and I've got an attentive audience, and there's a certain type of profession out there that knows that it is dealing with these issues but doesn't think about it, and then there's the rest of the world that consumes architecture, but finds architecture extremely difficult to connect with because of the language, the difficulty in reading a plan, let alone the combination of an impregnable discourse together with abstract models. So I was interested in how to take this idea, and how to exploit these totally diverse contingencies. What became interesting for me was combining the intellectual programme with a geographical spread. At that time, half the world was living in cities. So it was natural to look at them, and if we went big in terms of cities and the numbers of cities, we could also fill the space. I remember writing a sketch of how this exhibition would work, by choosing five regions of the world each with four cities, and explaining that this would be the layout for the space. But how does one talk about it and make sure it connects to architecture rather than social geography? I know there were people who saw the show and didn't like it, thinking that it was social geography and had nothing to do with architecture. I think that our most powerful decision, in the end, was to show architecture mainly as projections. I hadn't realised how powerful that graphic treatment was. I hadn't realised that an aerial image of Caracas at 5m, when well-lit, would take people's breath away.

AL: But was that a conscious decision on your part?

RB: I had anticipated it, but I hadn't anticipated that it would be so powerful, insofar as I had made the choice to show architecture and architectural projects in a relatively abstract way through a projector. In other words, there was a possibility to visit the exhibition without seeing architecture, though the architecture was there. When you've got these major themes to work with, you try to relate them to current concerns in architecture. But architecture today doesn't really engage with these issues yet. The projects that were featured have in many ways now got a life of their own, for instance the Urban Think Tank Project in Caracas. I opened up *Domus* last month and there was the Urban Think Tank with that cable car in Caracas. So it generated an interest, captured the imagination and infected what is today considered mainstream. There were four primary things that I sought to communicate in the exhibition: the density of populations; the speed of urban change over time; issues of violence, crime or segregation; issues of transportation and mobility; and how these themes affect the development of cities. Then there were questions such as: how is a city managed? How is a city governed? As things went on I just kept to these headlines. I had two people working full-time for the nine months who did the GIS work and mapped many of the graphs. Both of those elements have become the signature of what we did. You can talk about density but absolutely no one understands it as such except people in the field.

AL: By density, you mean tabular data in this case?

RB: Yes, an Excel spreadsheet. So we took that data and said, how can we relate this to another city? I think it was my graphic designer who said, 'You have to make models out of these'. And I said, 'But they're just abstract information', and she said, 'People are going to be amazed', and that led to the creation of that central room in the exhibition. Perhaps for the first 10 models you weren't thinking about the data, but then over the course of viewing the next 10 you couldn't help but think of it in this way: 'Did you see London, and how massively tall Cairo is?' And of course there are no green spaces in that model. This approach to the exhibition provided an interesting way of thinking about the planning of cities.

AL: Did you see the show as a form of research?

RB: Yes, in fact it kick-started an investigation. The research wasn't already there, it was absolutely generated by the show, so in that sense it is very much a research show. The issue of photography was also important. One had to find pictures that spoke in seconds about what these things were about, that visually linked and connected all these things.

AL: Did you think of your approach as a sort of exhibition methodology, an attempt to articulate another approach to the biennale?

RB: Sure. In a way, that was the first point I was making. Relating physical to social conditions was totally new. I don't think other shows have addressed that issue. So in this case my intention was very much to skew the discourse in a particular direction.

AL: Density had such a prominent role to play in the selection of cities featured in your exhibition. Were you tempted to direct attention to Venice itself, which is, after all, a dying city?

RB: No, not really. There is nothing like Venice. And unfortunately it is the anti-city. I did use Venice in the sense of providing a scale comparison of cities. I asked how many Venices fit inside Caracas, but that was a mathematical device.

AL: I understand that you were visualising data, but you were also relying on projection to tell another story. Can you talk more about that, and why you resorted to that rather cinematic approach?

RB: In the exhibition there were a variety of components to every city. For every city, I commissioned a filmmaker to go to the cities and make a short film of about three minutes to create a certain mood. I also commissioned a young group of video animators here in London to do an introductory film, which basically showed greater growth mixed with images of the cities. And I think that worked incredibly well in bringing people to understand what the context was. One of the other special things that we did was a 'density room' filled with the density models of each city. It was quite striking, as some were eight metres high or more.

AL: Did you meet a certain scepticism from a curatorial community that may have had other ideas about exhibitions, perhaps more indebted to ideas about display?

RB: Well in this show, the curator and his colleagues selected everything on the walls, and wrote every caption. In that sense it was a totally overdetermined experience, there was nothing democratic or open about it.

AL: But you weren't showing artists or architects. Instead you were raising questions and posing ideas. Wouldn't that be a radical shift from past biennales, in that you weren't showing with your biennale any artists or architects?

RB: Yes. In the last room, there were literally three massive boards with three questions.

AL: Am I correct in understanding that there was a different type of award during the year of your biennale, and that you gave the Golden Lion award to a city?

RB: That was one of the very first and very

obvious decisions that I made. If you're doing an exhibition on cities, then you give the Golden Lion to a city for the best city. I consider a city to be a great piece of design, so I don't see why one would not do this.

AL: You were very much addressing your biennale to the future, rather than the past, as was Hans Hollein with his biennale. Would you agree with that association?

RB: Sure, I think you can't be involved in this subject of cities without addressing the future. As it happens, the year I did the show was the year the world became more urban than not, and that statistic is a growing exponential. The world in 25 years will be two-thirds urbanised and architects will be building yet more and more. Is there going to be some sort of emerging model of urban form or architectural response which is socially and environmentally more sustainable?

AL: And while your exhibition was a spatial project, its reliance on data perhaps made it the easiest to document and archive. It lent itself practically to the form of the catalogue more than any earlier biennale. Would you agree that your catalogue provides accurate documentation of your show, or do you think there is something that evaded the catalogue?

RB: I wish I had two months to do the book again. You know our book *The Endless City*? That's how we should have done it. In the catalogue there's a combination of extremely strong images that were at the time not everyday occurrences, and there were some strong analytical texts, mainly urban anthropology. We diverged from other shows in that the catalogue was used as a resource for 18 or 20 schools of architecture, which then had a show in the last week. It meant that students from Turin could learn something about Mumbai, then go to Mumbai and conduct research and enact their project, then return to show it. And this happened.

AL: And this was reflected in the prize that you awarded for the best architectural school?

RB: Yes, and it worked out in a fantastic way. There were at least 500–600 students from all these schools, and they were there from the beginning. They went to other cities and then returned to spend a week in Venice. In that sense, it proved that the exhibition could provide an opportunity for genuine research.

AL: You toured the exhibition afterwards?

RB: Well, 200,000 to 300,000 people saw it in Venice overall. Then within six months

I had to recreate it for the Tate but it was completely different. That version was seen by 500,000 people. I had to transfer the ideas for the exhibition into a museum context, and that was interesting and the reaction was just as powerful. At the Tate we added cultural depth to it by working with artists who had worked in all these cities. I felt then, and recognise now, that it was the beginning of an ongoing project. Some people criticised that it was all like a book on the walls. But I think not. I mean, the president and I walked down the Arsenale a week before it opened, and he said 'Our audience likes walls.' And I said, 'I can assure you, your audience will like other things here.' Of course one is aware of the conventions of showing things. In this case we had to invent a new convention.

AL: What would you have liked to do differently?

RB: I certainly don't think we needed more time. Another three months and we'd have been dead! It's too much work and the scale is too big. I think the way we decided to display the architectural projects, and the amount of time and research we put into that as opposed to the rest, was wrong. We could have had some architectural models, why not? But the nice thing about this show is that it's all on a CD. I mean, the whole thing: the structures, the density model, the instructions. The other regret I have is the total lack of potential engagement with curators from other countries, which I found very frustrating. The French did this fantastic thing by inhabiting their building with a commune of artists. But it was all so hit or miss. This is something that on a structural level the biennale could consider.

AL: Some of the directors that preceded you have sought to leave things behind after their biennales. Dal Co left the James Stirling bookstore that he commissioned, for instance. Were you tempted to leave traces?

RB: I'm no architect, so it would have been presumptuous of me to try and do that. If the legacy is that these questions are addressed in subsequent shows, then that's good.

AL: I have one last question for you, which concerns the financial aspects of your exhibition. Was the budget that the biennale provided enough, or were you also responsible for fundraising?

RB: Yes, in a big way. I decided I would raise more money so I rose about a million and a half. I had to bring in someone for the opening party and pay £100,000. It's maybe the last thing you want to do when you haven't slept in six months! But it's fine.

Aaron Betsky

New York
Monday 12 April 2010

*Aaron Betsky directed 'Out There: Architecture
Beyond Building', the eleventh architecture exhibition
at the Venice Biennale. The exhibition, on display
from 14 September to 23 November 2008 in
the Arsenale and the Giardini, explored the idea that
architecture today cannot be practised in isolation, and
that art, literature, film, landscape architecture and
design have a vital role in the way we think about and
live in buildings.*

Aaron Levy and William Menking: We are
interested in the 2008 biennale that you curated,
'Beyond Building'. Could you explain what your
vision for the exhibition was, perhaps in relation to
your earlier writings such as *Architecture Must Burn
and Architecture Beyond Building*? How did these
ideas play out in Venice?

Aaron Betsky: Well, I got a call in December
of 2008 from my secretary saying, 'There's a
man called Mr Baratta who would like to talk
to you.' And I said, 'Who is he? What does he
want to talk about?' She said, 'I don't know;
it's something to do with the biennale.' I said,
'Okay. Give him my cell phone number.' Five

minutes later I get a call and he says, 'This is Paolo Baratta. I am president of the biennale, and I have a problem and perhaps you can help me. I was just appointed president, and my predecessor forgot to appoint a director of the architecture biennale. I don't have a curator and this exhibition opens about eight months from now.' And I said, 'Well, Mr Baratta, that's very interesting because I did the Dutch pavilion three times and I always thought that if you were going to do a biennale, what you really need to concentrate on is the spectacle. The great thing about the biennale is that whatever you think about it in moral or ethical terms, or even in terms of the truths of architecture, it is the *one* place where everyone in the world comes together to look at and think about what architecture is today, and it's even more true for art. And the biennale gets criticised – you can't ever do it right – but what it needs, and what it often lacks, is a spectacle to ground it – some sense that people really are here for this kind of explosion of colours and forms and textures that together offer a critical alternative to the banality of everything we already know.' And I went on like this for a few more minutes and there was a brief silence and then Baratta said, 'I think you have solved my problem.' And I said, 'Well, hold on a second. I have a day job and I'm not sure I can do this.' And he said, 'At least go look at the space.' So we arrive at the

Arsenale and one of the absolutely stellar staff, Massimiliano, meets us there on a very cold day, the day before Christmas. We walk up to the Arsenale, the Corderie, and open up the door. I had been there many times to see the art and architecture biennale, but I'd never seen the space empty. So, he opens up these huge wooden doors and there is half a mile of space – medieval, high-vaulted, brick-columned space, all completely empty. Peter, my partner, looks at me, looks at the space, looks at me, and says: 'Well, there goes 2008. What are we doing in 2009?' because you can't turn down the opportunity to fill that space.

To get a little bit more serious: I have done over a hundred exhibitions on architecture, and I'm not sure that any of them are any good. And that's because it is virtually impossible to make an exhibition of architecture. I think we can maybe have some interesting discussions about the terms, because the Italian word for an exhibition, *mostrare*, means not just to show but to reveal, to make public. And 'to unfold', of course, also has wonderful overtones. But in the West and in a traditional art museum, you usually have to put something on the pedestal, or in the frame. And the problem is that architecture usually resides in buildings and buildings don't usually fit inside other buildings. So what you wind up doing is having scale models or drawings of buildings that don't have any of the spatial sense of those buildings, drawings that only nerds like us understand; colour photographs that are these sappy, Disneyland versions of what, maybe, the buildings look like at sunset – but no sense of architecture. I had already been experimenting in previous years at SFMoMA with ways in which you could show architecture itself, and get at the essential qualities of architecture. I made what I thought was a very simple argument in my biennale, which perhaps was a disaster because I don't think anyone really understood it. I still think I'm communicating it clearly, but obviously I failed utterly. It was a simple argument: that the way you show architecture, perhaps, is not to show buildings, because architecture is not buildings. We think they are the same thing, but they are most definitely not. Buildings are buildings. They are objects, with spaces. Building is a verb, to build something. Architecture is everything that is about buildings. It's how we show buildings, how we draw buildings, how we design buildings, how we talk about buildings, how buildings appear to us; it's everything about buildings. Buildings are the most complete ways in which architecture can appear. But, these days especially, buildings are so much defined by issues outside of the discipline of architecture, that they more often than not become the tomb of architecture. Buildings are defined by codes: like safety codes, building codes, financial codes, codes of behaviour, computer codes. They're standardised, and there's very little you can do. Not only that, but even in a more general sense, if you were to bring someone in here who was not an architecture person and try to show them where the architecture is here, you would have to do a lot of dancing around to talk about the column that maybe represents structure, and the skylights, and to try to talk about spatial proportions. Eyes would glaze over almost immediately to anyone who's not an architecture nerd. Instead, where do you find architecture? Well, you find it in intentions, in dreams, and often in places where architecture is more fully realised, like movies and television. You find it in utopian visions. You find it also in interiors that are fully designed, which are more powerful as scene-setting environments than buildings. You find it outside of buildings, in landscapes which likewise have a greater power to control an environment. You find it all around buildings and beyond buildings. So, I said, 'Let us look beyond buildings to find architecture and to show it.'

WM: How much of this did you communicate to the architects that you were exhibiting? Or was it more a question of picking those architects and exhibitors who you thought could achieve this effect?

AB: There were two different ways that I picked the architects. And this is back to the question of the writings I have already done on the topic. For what was then called the Italian pavilion, which is about 20,000 square feet of white-box space in the Giardini, I made a survey of what I called experimental architecture. I have been interested for a while in what I call experimental architecture, which I think is a mode of making architecture that started appearing in the 1970s when people realised that utopia – the traditional escape valve for architects who did not want to be just part of a service profession – was 'precluded', and that one had instead to think of architecture as a way of experimenting on and in the world, the real world. And it started at places like the Institute for Architecture and Urban Studies in New York, and at the Architectural Association in London. I basically first put my students to work and explained what I meant by experimental architecture and said, 'Okay – go!' They turned on their computers and came back the next morning with hundreds of sites. Then I put a former colleague of mine at the Netherlands Architecture Institute, Emiliano Gandolfi, to work on disciplining that and finding other things – filling it, basically, with experiments from around the world. I only had six months to do the biennale, and my biggest regret is that I couldn't travel to see these things. So, it was very internet-based – a weakness in itself. For the Arsenale, I sent out a question to about three or four dozen architects who I respected and thought were doing experimental work. And that was: 'How can we take those systems that control our daily lives and that are mainly of a technological nature and how can we reveal them, appropriate them and domesticate them in such a manner that we can feel at home in the modern world?' And I put that question out and asked for proposals and out of the answers, selected about two dozen projects. I gave them each a little bit of money and they all spent about ten times as much and made installations in the Arsenale, and that's more or less how I filled it.

WM: Many of the installations had a kind of performative quality about them. Why did that happen? It's not unusual for the biennale to do that, but why did you take that trajectory? Aaron and I thought Gehry's and Diller, Scofidio and Renfro's gondola projects were among the most powerful. They had that kind of experiential quality about them. There's also a picture of you with your head in Coop Himmeb(l)au's installation 'Feed Back Space/Astroballon 1969 Revisited'. Can you speak about that piece in particular? That had never been built before, so it was presumably created especially for the biennale. What were you trying to get at by including that project from the 1960s?

AB: I think that what you want to do when you show architecture is to have an experience of architecture. Qualities of construction, of spatial manipulations and sequencing and composition, are all issues that you want to explore. And exploring them in a static sense is more difficult than activating them through installation or performance. Coop Himmelb(l)au was part of this discourse on experimental architecture. The firm's very name – 'The Cooperative of the Blue Way of Heaven' – was tied, in 1968 when it was formed, to the Paris revolutions and to the whole notion that we do not need to build a perfectly designed world, but we do need to liberate the unconscious. We need to liberate the body and social relations. Their experiments from that era were all about opening up a space within the city by burning things, by cutting holes, by attacking the static structures (both social and physical) around them. Some of their ideas were so wild they only existed as drawings. When I sent this call out, Wolf Prix got in touch with me and said, 'We have always dreamed of doing something like this, and now we think we have the technology to build it.' So, they did.

AL: I'm interested in your thoughts about working in Venice. It's hard not to be attentive to what's come before, and to feel that one has somehow to respond to that long history. As I listen to

148

you speak about your experiential and rather theatrical approach in the Arsenale I can't help but assume you were referencing Portoghesi's *Strada Novissima*?

AB: My great model was indeed the *Strada Novissima*, and if I had the money and the power I would have made something even more like the *Strada Novissima*.

AL: So you don't see the *Strada Novissima* as something that has passed, that represents a historical moment; you see it as one that has continued relevance.

AB: No, it's very much a historical moment in that it's facadism alone, where the architecture is reduced to a series of masks that present themselves in one dimension and the architects then just present their own little follies within that. I never saw it in real life, but what you get from the photographs and when you talk to people who were there is the spectacular sense of a new city emerging out of the darkness of the Arsenale: it was spectacular. My other big model was Aldo Rossi and his Theatre of the World, floating in the lagoon of Venice. Those were the kind of things I really wanted to try to achieve. I did see the biennale reacting to my predecessors, in the sense that Deyan Sudjic had tried to find architecture by reducing it to the nuggets of the best form, Kurt Forster tried to find the best ideas, Ricky Burdett tried to find the economic infrastructure and social infrastructure for that. I felt like they had surveyed the field and now it was time to kick out the jams, to do something that showed what was possible beyond the kind of clarity and sometimes depressing truths that they had revealed.

AL: Francesco Dal Co had of course commissioned the Stirling bookstore. And Kurt Forster shared with us, when we interviewed him, his unfulfilled dream of having the landscaping of the Giardini redone. You clearly commissioned various installations in the Giardini and elsewhere: did you have aspirations to do something of that sort, something that would leave a residue?

AB: One of the first things I suggested was that we redo the Giardini and they all laughed and said, 'Every director says that.'

AL: How did you want to redo it?

AB: As a set of projects. I said, well, we need a garden that is a Garden of Eden. So I called Kathryn Gustafson and took her out to the kind of left-over garden that's all the way at the end of the Arsenale, the Garden of the Virgins, and she found this unclaimed piece of ruined garden, which became her project, to renovate it into half a prototype for how we could turn our cities into places for urban gardening and half into a really utopian, beautifully abstracted space surmounted by helium balloons representing all of us going to Heaven. And Baratta and the organisation kept it and built a bridge at the back of the garden which reconnects the Arsenale right to the centre of Castello, the neighbourhood between the Arsenale and the Giardini, so that you now have a shortcut right into that part of town. I'm very proud of that, because I think it's something that we left behind for future biennales to enjoy.

WM: Aaron and I talked to Kazuyo Sejima about her ideas and she mentioned how she is reacting to the ubiquity of architecture in the age of the internet. How do you think that the internet and the display of architecture in a virtual world has changed the actual practice of staging exhibitions?

AL: On a related note, you have remarked elsewhere about feeling like you are done with exhibitions. Was the biennale in a certain sense like a last attempt in an age of increasing virtualisation?

AB: Maybe – it was certainly the largest exhibition that I'm likely ever to get to do. So, what do you do after that? I think there are two questions here: one is about the internet and one is about exhibitions. The interesting thing about the internet is that it takes away the novelty that biennales once had. Traditionally, one of the reasons you would schlep from wherever you were to Venice, or to the Whitney Museum of Art, or to the Carnegie, or to any of these kind of events was that it was your chance to see things from all over the world. And now, each of us, every morning, as we have our coffee and in between phone calls, surf 40 or 50 sites and everything that anyone from Chile to Timbuktu is doing is on the internet within a day or two – it's very rare that you find something that manages to remain hidden from that power. So the internet is like a continual biennale; everything is continually on display. On the one hand, this makes it easier, because it means you have a better chance of finding interesting work from around the world that you might otherwise miss; I think that shouldn't be underestimated. And, if you find someone interesting and then give them a chance to do something really great, that's a positive thing. I think it also puts pressure on you, because it's not enough for someone just to show their stuff, because you could see it on your screen. You have to let them do something that would make it be worth going there physically to see it.

That sort of also answers the question about exhibitions. People complain about the need for exhibitions to be more and more spectacular. Yes – and what is wrong with that? Art itself is putting more and more emphasis on its own experiential qualities or is finding ways of integrating itself with community and media in a way that is completely disseminated. The medium of the exhibition is either exploding out into the street or becoming a site where the most amazing objects and spaces are collected and surrounded with an elaborate framework that heightens your experience of them. It is forcing exhibitions to try to understand what their essence is, what they're about, and I think there's nothing wrong with that.

I'm come to the conclusion that we tend to think of museums as machines for making exhibitions, but they're not. Museums, art museums, are machines for bringing people and art together. At the Cincinnati Art Museum, I've changed our mission statement, so that's what it now says. The museum brings the people of the greater Cincinnati, northern Kentucky area and great art together. Period – end of it. You then have to ask the question: what is the best way to do that? And it turns out that doing standard exhibitions is a very expensive way; it's almost impossible to do a decent art exhibition for less than a few hundred thousand dollars these days. Given the financial limits, space limits and every other limit – I think it's much better for us to concentrate on developing new ways.

WM: We've talked about Gehry and Coop Himmelb(l)au and Diller, Scofidio and Renfro. Which other ones really stood out for you in the Arsenale building?

AB: I think I'm the only one who really liked Nigel Coates' installation *Hypnerotosphere*, which people were somewhat critical about. I thought it was a very beautiful way of looking at architecture as something that occurs not as the making of objects but as a relationship between bodies and buildings and between buildings and cities, where you're trying to find a sensuality rather than a kind of harsh criticality.

AL: I have two different questions. The first one calls our attention back to Kurt Forster's ninth Venice architecture biennale. He talked about how the Italian government cut the show's budget, which was already spaghetti-thin, forcing him to become 'a beggar on every corner in Europe'. He had to postpone the opening when it coincided with the Venice Film Festival. In every sense, he found himself caught up in what seemed to be a logistical nightmare. Did you have a different experience?

AB: Very different. He had the worst of it, because he had a difficult administration. I had president Baratta and Andrea Del Mercato, who was a fantastic executive director, and Manuela

154

Luca Dazio, who is now the head of the architecture section. Of course there was not enough money to do things, and of course there's bureaucracy. But when I gave up trying to be an architect many years ago and decided to organise stuff, I learned that organising stuff always involves confronting these kinds of difficulties and, given the scale of the operation, they were not nearly as large as I had feared. It was easier for me than for the architects. I had to explain to the architects who would run in optimistically and say, 'We'll do this.' I'd say, 'Remember little things like the fact that the cost of shipping a container full of material from Shanghai to Mestre, the port of Venice, is the same as the cost of then getting the material from Mestre into the biennale. It's a very complicated situation – not my problem, their problem. Once you understand those parameters, it wasn't nearly as difficult as I'd thought.

Two things to understand. First of all Italy, as a country, is interested in and supports architecture, and once you work with the press, and they get excited, for or against, it means that things have to happen. And the press in Italy is a wonderful weapon for getting things done. I had a lot of fun working with that. The second is that Venice is an incredible draw: I mean, people will do almost anything to be in Venice and to show their work in Venice and to be part of the Venice Biennale because they know that 200,000 people will see it and it will be in all the newspapers and so the ability to leverage those qualities is one of the things that I think makes a biennale very doable. The budget is not nearly enough, but it is more than any other situation I've ever worked in.

AL: Gregotti and Francesco Dal Co in particular cautioned us: they said that you can't understand the history of the biennale just by looking at the curatorial manifestation – instead you have to understand the political climate of the board of overseers, and things like that. Did that not impact you, just as in an earlier historical moment it had impacted them?

AB: I met the board of overseers twice. And that was it. I met Cacciari, the mayor of Venice, who was a great philosopher, which was a real honour for me. But, as I said, Paolo Baratta was extremely helpful. The trick, again, was the press.

WM: I don't understand that – how does that make things happen? No one has told us that yet in all of our interviews.

AB: If you say things in a way that are provocative without being obnoxious and you manage to get one or two of the key critics to agree with you, it creates a lot of public interest, and a lot of debate back and forth. And then, from my perspective and what I understand from talking to people, the board of overseers are happy if they get the sense that the biennale is seen as being alive – having something that people are angry or miffed or just worried about is as good as people being excited. The last thing you want is for it to be boring and completely noncommittal. I didn't even have to do anything. When my name was announced, Gregotti wrote an editorial for *Corriere della Sera*, I think, denouncing my appointment and saying how terrible it was going to be. I hadn't even said what I was going to do! So I decided that two could play at that game, and when they asked me what I thought of it at my first press conference I said, 'Well, he can say what he wants. As far as I'm concerned, he's an irrelevant architect. I've learned more about Italian architecture from Bernardo Bertolucci or Michelangelo Antonioni than I ever did from Gregotti.' And that got a lot of press. Then a good debate started, and a few very interesting critics came to see me and had serious questions. The interesting thing about my biennale was that the Italian press on the whole loved it in the end; the foreign press hated it. I think it's a record. I was panned on the same day in the most important papers – *El País* in Spain, the *Frankfurter Allgemeine* in Germany, *Le Monde*

157

in France, *The Guardian* in England and the *LA Times*, with *The New York Times* adding its own insult by refusing to even review it – all on the same day. It was devastating, but I sort of knew it was going to happen.

WM: Why did the Italians like it?

AB: Because I said that architecture is not just about making buildings, it is a social activity, a way of understanding where we are and who we are. There's a kind of sclerotic, historic preservation-based mafia that controls most major construction in Italy and by attacking them head-on it created interest and debate.

AL: I want to go back to the story of the shipping container that costs as much to get from Shanghai to Mestre as it does from Mestre to the Giardini. I'm particularly interested in sharing with the public those stories, because they impact so much of what you see. Is the notion of sharing these logistics with the public of interest to you? Or is that precisely what a show is not supposed to display?

AB: I think of logistics as a reality of modernity. Modernity is, in the end, as Marshall Berman said years ago, 'no more than the continual movement of people, goods and information'. In fact, I really wanted to do a second biennale exploring ways of displaying that. I was going to call it 'Shrink Wrap' and it was going to be about the reduction of all reality to the most condensed things, the containerisation of things, having them in wrappers, and I was going to build this project with MVRDV which was to be a huge pavilion made out of shipping containers that you could stack up eight high and make a huge space – but some other time. If anyone has a couple of million dollars, I have the plans ready, I'll do it. That interests me. And the other thing that interests me is the notion of construction, of making things. Frank Gehry's installation I also thought was very, very beautiful because he went back to something he said years ago, which is: a building under construction is much more beautiful than when it's finished, and showed a building as scaffolding, which again is something Colin Rowe talked about – for me, the essence of *Collage City* is not the collage, but when he talks about scaffolding.

AL: I want to go back to the Netherlands Architecture Institute and your long, 25-year engagement in research and education. Did you see that as something that should play out in your biennale? Was the EveryVille competition your idea? Was it Baratta's? Could you talk about the degree to which you saw the biennale as an educational opportunity that should either engage students or be addressed to students?

AB: It's one of the failures of the biennale. I think it's not just my failure. I think Ricky Burdett was the only one who started to really get students involved because he really built his biennale out of universities. In the case of my biennale, the EveryVille competition was organised around a series of known universities around the world that did research, that did projects, and they all came together to make the heart of the biennale. We had very little time for an educational component when we came up with this competition. It didn't work very well. We didn't get enough people to know about it. That, for me, was one of the failures of the biennale; however, I'm not sure how you can do that better. Baratta's dream, which I think a fantastic one, is to make the Venice Biennale into a permanent institute that periodically produces the various presentations but also creates a kind of research and development institute that is a permanent centre for the study of the history and future of the built environment. I sort of dream of it as a kind of architectural equivalent of Princeton's Institute of Advanced Studies, and if he ever pulls it off, I think it would be great, it would be absolutely spectacular. But I think that a biennale or an exhibition is not the best place to show student work, in general. I think that there is a skill to presenting, which is what you do in a show like that, that is learned and though students can be wonderfully exuberant and sometimes do great stuff, it also takes a certain amount of experience and discipline to build up the ability to show things in a spectacular way.

AL: We find ourselves in a moment when curating is becoming professionalised and institutionalised in a way that perhaps hasn't happened before: you can get a degree in curating.

AB: I'm waiting to see the real results of curating programmes, so I don't really know what they're going to produce. It is a very weird thing because, traditionally, there has been no way to learn how to be a curator. And there *really* has been no way to learn how to be a curator in the fields of architecture and design. It is fantastic that the Cooper Hewitt and some other places are trying to make that a more open and clear path. On the other hand the notion of curating is changing even as we speak – people are now talking (there was an article in *The New York Times* a few days ago) about 'curating' dance performances. It's becoming a more malleable word, so I'm not sure if the programmes will be able to keep up with the mutations in the field.

AL: What's so fascinating about the Venice Biennale is that is has the most remarkable archives and yet they're also, perhaps, the most difficult to access. I was wondering if you had spent any time in the archives. When we spoke to Baratta, he'd explained that your biennale had been a particularly difficult one for them, from the archival perspective, because your biennale played out on a BlackBerry. Does all correspondence carry the same archival weight? How do you archive a BlackBerry? It wasn't even their BlackBerry, it was not their property; it was yours.

AB: In fact, I could not have done that biennale without modern technology. Yes, archiving modern material is becoming very difficult and, of course, in the world of architecture more and more of what we produce is digital, and so what is it that you preserve? I was the first person, as far as I know, to make websites part of a permanent collection of an art museum when I was in San Francisco. I kept saying to them, 'These websites are free', and they pointed out to me that in order to maintain a website in an archival manner – meaning that you should be able to experience them 200 years from now in the manner in which they were designed – cost, in 1999, $20,000 a year per website because you have to keep it running, continually, with backups. It's a huge job. So it's a very big issue.

AL: How did you document your biennale?

AB: I didn't.

AL: But clearly the publication that you oversaw was one attempt at that. Kazuyo Sejima told us that she's planning something very small and simple and compact. Your publication was not. Wouldn't that be an archival manoeuvre?

AB: We came up with the idea of not making a singular catalogue. I also felt, since I am rather strident in my beliefs, that you needed manifestos, and I commissioned manifestos that we collected in the book. In the end you had five different publications that together made up a kind of sprawling biennale documentation. One of the things I've found is that my photographs of the biennale are awful, and the biennale's are worse than mine.

AL: And the photographs would be the way that you would want your biennale in history to be perceived and understood?

AB: Right – and little QuickTime movies...

Kazuyo Sejima

New York
Friday 5 March 2010

Kazuyo Sejima directed 'People Meet in Architecture', the twelfth architecture exhibition at the Venice Biennale. The exhibition, on display from 29 August to 21 November 2010 in the Arsenale and the Giardini, explored the essential role of architecture and the importance of recognising relationships between individuals within their social and natural environments.

Aaron Levy and William Menking: You have a long history with the Venice Biennale. In 2000 you curated the Japanese pavilion, and in 2004 you received the Golden Lion award. Has this history, and your attentiveness to the biennale as an institution, informed what you're doing as director in 2010? Or is that history of prior engagement of no concern in your present work?

Kazuyo Sejima: I have had a chance to participate in two or three biennales. Those times that I was invited to participate together with my partner, Ryue Nishizawa, I was simply asked to send models. The exhibition had a theme, and I had no idea how they would present my project. I only visited the exhibition briefly, and it was difficult to see and understand everything. I just went to see my project, and to make sure the model was not broken! This experience was somehow a starting point for me to think about the 2010 biennale. This time with my biennale, apart from providing the theme, I thought it might be better not to overload visitors with information – in part because information now reaches everyone so quickly via the internet anyway. Perhaps the more important thing is to meet people and experience the projects, to have some sort of contact with the materials on display. I am giving each participant one space, and encouraging them to create some sort of atmosphere with the few materials available. But it is very difficult – there are so many monetary limitations, and the biennale spaces are so huge – so we are still struggling with how to display the work. But basically the starting point for our exhibition is that there are 20 rooms in the International Pavilion and 13 in the Arsenale. I will perhaps vary the rooms, so that there is not just one architect operating under one theme. Ideally the public can have different types of experiences, and can feel the different atmosphere made by each exhibitor.

WM: Does that mean the projects will all be connected and presented as a single exhibition, or will they be presented as separate instalments?

KS: Just now, we are in the period where we are engaging in conversation with each of the participants, and it is difficult to construct relations between them! But at the same time, the exhibit shouldn't be boring. There will be some very intense projects in the show, and then others that are very quiet, and yet others that are even quieter. Of course the participants we are speaking with would like to know which space they will be given, but if there are two busy rooms next to each other, well, then we will say to them: please propose a solution. If the space that each one would like to use won't work for their needs, then we ask them: 'How about this?' We are trying to control the rhythm of the show, rather than the conceptual connections, so that it kind of goes, 'busy, busy, rest'. It's all kind of open.

AL: So the exhibition will in a sense take the form of a conversation?

KS: Yes.

AL: And in your planning process, the exhibition unfolds over time and involves each of the participants.

KS: Yes. So, we cannot decide things too quickly and nor can the architects.

AL: Would it be appropriate to say that your exhibition is a response to earlier biennales that you feel did not take this, lets say, conversational and processual form? We know that you have been in conversation with Vittorio Gregotti, Francesco Dal Co and other directors recently. Do you see your approach as different – not a critique in a negative sense, but a different approach to theirs?

KS: I don't know all the history, although I understand that recently several curators have focused on cities and other such topics. So this year I want to focus on the building itself. But of course buildings need context, so that means that someone must show something related to the city. Throughout this process, I often like to react, and not to decide. This is the conversational approach that you are talking about. For the biennale I chose the title 'People Meet in Architecture'. I realise it is a very difficult title, but the whole project is not easy to describe. When I selected the participants, I asked each of them to think about this title. I always want to say that architecture should always be open to the public. And I hope the people I have invited to participate in this biennale are interesting, and interested in that.

WM: The biennale usually represents what's new in the world of architecture. What criteria did you use in deciding who to invite?

KS: I tried to invite a younger generation, but now so many people know each other through the computer or through travelling, and it's not at all difficult to find or to meet young people! I think that today everybody, because of the internet, is already famous! And since I am not so good at using the internet, I always find out that oh, no, this person who is new to me is already famous. There are still so many things on the table. So much stuff printed out, so much stuff sent, so many conversations. If it sort of feels relevant – to architecture, to the world – not to the theme, particularly, but just on the most basic level, then we try to take it further, and if possible, to ask for proposals. I have asked Yuko Hasegawa to be a curatorial advisor. I worked with her for the Twenty-first-Century Museum of Contemporary Art in Kanazawa, and now she has moved to MoT in Tokyo as their chief curator. I also asked my partner Ryue Nishizawa to be a curatorial advisor. Our team, including Sam Chermayeff, Jack Hogan and Satoshi Ikeda, meets often. Mostly, we just discuss things. We discuss inviting different people, including architects, engineers and also a few artists. I wanted to invite a few engineers and artists to show some work through the form of collaborations.

AL: Your selection approach is somewhat intuitive, then?

KS: Yes, for sure.

WM: Have you approached curating the Arsenale and the Italian pavilion differently?

KS: We discussed the difference between the Italian pavilion and the Arsenale, but in the end we've treated them the same way. Some works shine more in a white gallery, while some do better in the Arsenale. Other works feature materials best suited to a much darker space, while in other cases, it's white on white. Our approach in this project is always to ask, for example, 'How about this, or maybe this?' With each of the proposals, we must change each thing, and everything happens in response to everything else.

WM: The Arsenale is so linear, and curators usually put everything off to the side or treat the space as an installation in response to that. With Asymptote, for instance, Kurt Forster created a meandering line through the Arsenale; with Portoghesi, the *Strada Novissima* created a straight line like a street straight through the space. What are your current thoughts about the space and your approach to the exhibition?

KS: We are not using money for the design of the exhibition, and will try instead to give money to the architects, and ask them how to use the space. The money is limited and the space is big, so it's really not enough. For example, to give a sense of our process: we have a given space, and one architect will show a few things in that space. We will think with them about how to put things together, and then this will determine ultimately the kind of experience, give it a kind of continuity.

WM: The Italian pavilion is very different.

KS: It is not one space; instead it has many directions and paths. In other words, it is not conclusive. As a result, we are thinking of showing big-scale structure models, or solo shows and small studies, or else photographs, or... Many different things.

WM: Yes, the Italian pavilion is very strange because they have rooms both above and below ground. One of our other questions for you concerns the possibility of bringing universities and students into the biennale. Is this important to you, and is it a priority with your biennale?

KS: It's not about showing things. It's about engaging students with the experience of the exhibition. It's not particularly about asking them to contribute materials, but to experience it.

171

AL: Philosophically, do you believe that the biennale needs to be more pedagogical or more didactic? Do you feel that the exhibit, in a way, should be placed more directly in the service of teaching?

KS: The first time I came to the biennale I was not a student but an exhibitor and I didn't know how to communicate with other people, or even how to see the whole thing. But I'm hoping that a lot of students will come, and that they will also be a part of the biennale. It has become a good opportunity to start to think about architecture, and to help them to connect. For this reason, we hope to do a conference during the biennale that asks 'what is architecture education?' In addition, the official plan of the biennale is that every Saturday the director of a past biennale will come back and quietly discuss their exhibition.

AL: One of our other questions concerns Venice itself. In a way, in organising the US pavilion, we felt we were in competition with the city, because many people come to the Giardini and the Arsenale with the same sort of expectations they bring to Venice, which is such a spectacular site. There is a spectacular logic and a sense of economic tourism that has perhaps invaded or defines the public's relation to the biennale. Do you think about Venice in this way?

KS: We never talk about it, and I didn't think about it! But I think the one reason that some people still have some expectations of the biennale is that the city of Venice is so special. I think we are competing, perhaps not explicitly, with the city, and that it is important that when people visit the exhibit they respond with a certain degree of 'wow'. Because the biennale is so big, it is a spectacle. And because the internet, and books, cover the biennale's history and architecture in general, there are more smart people around thinking about architecture than I'd realised. Thus to go back to spectacle is maybe okay.

AL: Is exhibiting art and architecture the same thing? Do you feel that one can show a building in the way that one shows an artwork?

KS: I have been to the art biennale three times, and while artists show the artwork itself, in an architecture exhibition we cannot use the real thing – the building. Therefore in an architecture exhibition we have to think about how to show architectural quality. Even if someone makes a model, one-to-one scale, we are still not dealing with context. I ask every participant to show a model, together with each room's context, to create something. They must think about how it would be possible to show a project, albeit within the existing walls and conditions.

WM: This would be a departure, then, from Betsky's biennale, which was about an architecture beyond building, so to speak. You, on the contrary, want to return the focus back onto architecture.

KS: I am sorry if I am not being clear, but the title of my exhibition is 'People Meet in Architecture'. I have an image of the current society we live in and role that architecture has to play. I am thinking right now about how we make architecture today, as compared to the past, when an architect was a kind of grand master in charge of everything. That's impossible now, both in daily business and also in how one works with so many other professionals – engineers, designers, etc. I wouldn't say that either approach is good or bad. But this new way of making architecture also gives architecture a new quality, or character. And sometimes collaborations can help generate new styles of architecture.

AL: So are you inviting some of the architects and others you are featuring to collaborate?

KS: Yes. There are three or four sets of collaborators right now, maybe there will be a few more. For instance, sometimes there is a live person collaborating with a dead person, and thinking about history. I hope to be able to cultivate some new experiences. But we will not show things that are so exact that they still need qualification. Rather, we will try to show the ways of participation.

AL: It seems that everyone has such high aspirations for exhibitions today – we want exhibitions to change the world, to enact a certain politics, etc.

KS: I think I want to simply make an exhibition that will bring people closer together to think, to see lots of things, and to have a chance to talk about them. I want to provide a greater connection between the viewer and the exhibition itself.

AL: Have you curated other exhibitions in the past?

KS: Well, at SANAA we've curated our own exhibitions and done exhibition designs, but we have never selected participants like we are doing now.

AL: Are you excited by the possibilities of doing curation?

KS: Of course. Building is a conversation with the user, the client or the programme itself. And to design a small house or to build a big museum somehow exemplifies the same approach. I don't think there is that much difference for us between designing projects and curation.

WM: Working in Venice is particularly difficult; financial limitations and the short amount of time can be very frustrating.

KS: From a monetary point of view it's true, it's maybe too concentrated in time, it happens too quickly and there is too much to do.

AL: Do you mean you wish you could work with a smaller space, for instance just the Arsenale?

KS: Yes, from a monetary point of view, or from the point of view of time. It would be better, smaller and certainly easier to curate!

WM: You alluded to this before, but what is the role of the biennale in a technological age, in an age of increasing virtualisation?

KS: There are so many biennales and triennales now, though for me personally the Venice Biennale is the most famous. Even though you can see nice photographs of models on the internet, at the biennale one should really be able to see the real thing. It's a chance for less information and more feeling.

AL: Have you thought about the catalogue? Will it

document the exhibition, or display the work of the featured architects?

KS: We're trying to make it smaller and a little bit less cumbersome than in the past. We envision a small guide used as an index to the bigger catalogue, which will have reduced pages and be more specific, rather than creating some sort of rule where everybody gets two pages and has a set amount of text. It must be freer, because we're inviting participants to do quite different things that are leading us in several different directions. So we're trying to keep it very open, and looser, but also kind of contained. Where necessary, we are showing things in situ, meaning what they're actually making for the biennale.

WM: I think the past Venice Biennale catalogues have been an afterthought. Maybe it's time and money once again, but they seem to be printed at the last moment, as a form of documentation.

KS: Hopefully this one can be, first and foremost, something that you can deal with, and that doesn't feel like a list. Rather than a catalogue, hopefully it will feel more like a book somehow.

AL: Will there be a discursive aspect?

KS: Yes, I want there to be some kind of critique in the book, and for the participants to write something that will help the public think differently about architecture and questions of beauty. I am an architect, so I would like people to feel the possibility of architecture. But I want short and contained texts, not texts referencing everything. I want a few texts addressing overall issues, rather than each participant's explanation, which we will try to keep kind of small. And, obviously, we will try to make the design and printing seem a little bit nicer, so that whatever you look at seems important on that page. I thought at first to reduce the number of participants, but at the same time I was very worried that I could not show the diversity that exists today. There are some Venice Biennale catalogues that show only the top architects and projects in the exhibition, and others that show everything. I worry, as I don't think I can show everything. I wish we could spend more time on it.

WM: How early does it have to go to print?

KS: It goes to print at the end of the first week of August, and it's done two weeks later.

AL: The biennale is not just an exhibition but also an archive, one that keeps growing and changing over time. When we spoke with Paolo Baratta he explained how complex it is today to document how it all comes to be. Do you feel that you need to document not just what you show at the end of the day, but the process of curating what you show?

KS: We don't really. I mean, we keep all the drawings that are sent to us by the participants. But it's not like we are having a BlackBerry-generated discussion, it's all very literal. So there are drawings on the wall and drawings on the table, and there are little cutouts of various architects with little strings. It's a process that you can see at any point playing out, now, here. So we do document that, but I don't know what's going to happen with it all. I don't know what to do with all this material.

Paolo Baratta

Rome
Friday 18 December 2009

Paolo Baratta is the president of the Venice Biennale (1998–2000, 2007–). The directors of the biennale that he has appointed include Massimiliano Fuksas (2000), Deyan Sudjic (2002), Aaron Betsky (2008) and Kazuyo Sejima (2010).

Aaron Levy and William Menking: You have been the president of the Venice Biennale for some years now. But let's go back to your first biennale, with Massimiliano Fuksas. Why did you select him for the first architecture exhibition of your presidency?

Paolo Baratta: I must admit that he did exactly what I expected from him, which was to break up the idea of an exhibition composed of maquette after maquette and introduce something that was an invention by itself: a street down the centre of the Corderie. This may have resulted in it being too much of an exhibition based on the work of the curator, but this seems to me the problem with architecture exhibitions. What is an exhibition of architecture, particularly one like the Venice Biennale which started out as an art exhibition, with the same sort of criteria? The answer is that an exhibition of

architecture is in itself a contradiction. In art
exhibitions you show a work of art, whereas in
architecture you don't show the product of the
architect. So what do you show? Is an exhibition
of architecture at best only an indirect exhibition? Fuksas was really the first curator of
the biennale to understand this problem, and
he made the Corderie into a long street that
expresses a visual experience, so as to think
about architecture. His exhibition of architecture brought me to another set of questions.
Is an exhibition an instrument of knowledge
or documentation, or an emotional experience,
and do you play on the capacity of emotions to
introduce people to knowledge? Knowledge
through emotions is the language of any exhibition. And an exhibition has to take into account
that it is an instrument of knowledge and of
communication with its own rules, its own instruments, and its own logic. But there is no
recipe for this unsolved question. Even in
contemporary art it's a problem. I remember
my first art biennale with Harald Szeemann.
We were talking about what he was going to
do in the newly restored Arsenale. I explained
to him that we now had two spaces which were
completely different in nature: the traditional
Padiglione Italia (now called the Palazzo delle
Esposizioni), which has white walls, and is similar to any sort of museum or contemporary
Kunsthalle; and the Arsenale, which is a theatre,

a place where you have to imagine things as you cannot just put anything in there. My test of the quality of a curator is always the Corderie, because it is the most impossible space – it's madness. You have time, space and the exhibition itself, with its own emotional language. I must admit that I have been in exhibitions there – I won't tell you which ones, of course! – where I felt that the curator didn't play the instruments in the right way. It was as if they was playing the violoncello like a flute, or with the wrong bow. I also remember I made some mistakes myself in the beginning.

WM: Hearing you speak about Fuksas' exhibition makes me think of Portoghesi's *Strada Novissima* of 1991, which set a similarly very high standard for display in the Arsenale. Can you speak about that exhibition and what it means to you today?

PB: Portoghesi understood that you have to make an exhibition that is coherent with that extraordinary space. It was not the details of the *Strada Novissima* that were relevant for architects at the time, but more the idea that you have to start thinking about the city from the perspective of tradition and history again, and possibly give tradition new dramatic forms. The Corderie confirms that an exhibition can be a stage-set for an idea, a way of transmitting a concept or an emotion. The maquettes were there to inform you, to give you the possibility of seeing something you wouldn't otherwise see. It is interesting to think of this in relation to the experience of the internet, which is just information. Digital images of buildings are too easy to achieve today, and with regard to the biennale, there is no point in architects from all over the world seeing things that can be seen on the internet. Moreover, the public who comes to the architecture biennale is very important. Only half of this public belongs to the world of architecture, and an exhibition has to speak to those who are not in the discipline. I state this issue very strongly when I speak to curators. To Aaron Betsky, who sent me a paper of concepts, I said 'No, no, no.' This is not a book or an essay, it is theatre. And if you take the theatre of the Corderie and put things in it that are possibly not significant in themselves, it is a problem. You have sometimes to receive messages in an indirect way, and not necessarily in a direct way. I must say that Betsky did understand and apply this principle. Those were not pieces of architecture, but rather pieces of gaiety. It was a sort of theatre, and one might say that it was the dawn. In Betsky's biennale, one enters the world before architecture, and forms appear that might belong to the world of architecture or not. It's an aurora, and that's a very powerful idea.

AL: Paolo Portoghesi's *Strada Novissima* was a different model, in a certain sense. It was an attempt to provoke and be provocative, no?

> PB: It was a competitive model, because Portoghesi wanted to provoke architects. But Betsky also wanted to provoke ordinary visitors with the idea that architecture was something that you could understand and be part of. You didn't need technical knowledge, and if you abandoned yourself to this sort of experience of emotions you were brought into the world of architecture.

AL: If you look at the early architecture biennales, they are very much engaging a specialised audience of architects, and concerned with a different definition of what the public is or can be.

> PB: Once I completed the restoration of 17,000 square metres of the Arsenale, it was no longer sufficient to address the world of architects. That was what we were doing with Fuksas, an exhibition of architecture not only for architects or students, but for the public.

AL: In our conversation with Francesco Dal Co, it was quite clear that he saw the architecture biennale as an opportunity not just to show architecture, but also to renovate buildings and commission new structures – which in his case was the Stirling bookstore. In a certain way you've adopted that idea, but transposed it onto the biennale as an institution.

PB: When I stepped in as president of the biennale for a second time, I wanted to increase the role of architecture at the biennale. I gave it a big boost by making a major investment in restoring the Arsenale. The Corderie was already in use at the time, but not the whole Arsenale.

AL: You have also just upgraded and opened the archives of the biennale to the public and scholars?

PB: The archive is a problem with no solution. And if you leave the problem of the archive to those who are specialists in archives, well, you are lost. You have to invent a solution for it! First it's a historic archive and there have been mixed thoughts in the past about its role, and about how it should be organised. Should it be an archive of modern art, or focus instead on the history of the biennale itself? Then, of course, if you have the money, and if you have an intelligent librarian, you can always add something that is missing. But that has not been done, so you have to simply work on the level of fine-tuning the accumulation of documents. My opinion is that an institution like the biennale should focus on its own historical archive, and not pretend to have an archive of modern art which is beyond the reach of this institution. While its official title is 'Archive of Contemporary Art', because for a decade we started collecting as if we were building an archive of contemporary art, we just don't have the money. And unfortunately, having lost time and money pretending to make a historical archive, we didn't pay sufficient attention to the historical archive of the biennale itself. It's stupid to go around buying books for a collection of things with no specific meaning. The archive has gone through completely different and difficult experiences, because some authors and artists have also left us with specific gifts. Now we are giving priority to the documentation of our own activity. In this context, this year we are taking the James Stirling bookshop in the Giardini – which is somewhat like an old piece of beautiful furniture in that you don't really know what to do with it – and using it as a 'bibliography' for the biennale for the first time, asking each different artist to send books which speak about them. And this is a way of building up the library of the biennale. The Stirling pavilion will become the place where all these books donated by the artists and different architects will be at the disposal of the public, and then they will be deposited into the library. This is how you can build a library for the biennale.

WM: Does the archive have things that go all the way back to the foundation of the biennale in the nineteenth century?

PB: Yes, letters and so on are the core of the archive, and the most important of the collection because they are our history. Then, of course, you have second and third layers of documents that are related to the things that have happened in the different biennales. There is always the risk of building up something in the archive which might get out of control, and we don't have the money or the space to do that. We need to make changes, such as one that we initiated last year: every single director, as part of their duties, has to collect all the documents that are considered relevant to their year, and they are asked to spend some time collecting them. Then there is a formal procedure to bring it into the archive. This of course is becoming very difficult with the internet and with email, because with the BlackBerry device, for instance, you leave behind a lot of information which is possibly highly biased, whereas in an archive the interesting things are those that are not biased, or are there by chance. You discover that there has been a quarrel, and that there were problems. With BlackBerrys and email we have instruments of information that are too easy to delete and cancel. Now of course if you have a thousand emails dealing with 'oh, are you coming? I'm waiting...' it would be an absolutely useless archive. It's a paradox: it was all clearer and more obvious when the curators were writing a few letters a month, now it's not clear what we can get.

WM: Vittorio Gregotti explained that in the year of his biennale the architectural community was very small, and there wasn't a large public. He personally knew everyone featured in the exhibition, and the audience was primarily composed of those coming from the United States and Europe, Italy in particular.

PB: To some extent, there is still a small community at the opening. About 9,000 to 10,000 belong to that community. And some of them bring their friends or the persons with whom they have some relation, be they critics, artists or donors. Actually, there is still this sort of community belonging to the world of architecture, but the audience has of course grown.

AL: How do you respond to the desire today on the part of younger nation-states to establish their own pavilions?

PB: As an institution, the biennale cannot simply add new buildings because after restoring the Arsenale there is no surplus money for new buildings and, moreover, the local authorities have placed restrictions on doing so in the Giardini after the Stirling pavilion. That was the end of it, there will be no more pavilions there. But we are trying to bring different countries like China into the Arsenale to have their own pavilions, and hoping to restore other buildings there as well. The national pavilions belong to states that are officially recognised by the Italian government, but today we have so many participating that are not officially recognised, and each wants its own space. In the Arsenale there are a lot of spaces that still have to be restored. When you pass the Corderie, there is an area of 3,500 square metres that is in a very bad condition but can be restored. You could have six pavilions of 500 square metres each, which is a decent size. We often host countries and regions within other parts of the Arsenale, such as China, Abu Dhabi and Latin America. The idea of having national pavilions at the biennale, which began more than 150 years ago, may be somewhat obsolete today. But once I restored the Arsenale, this phenomenon of the national exposition returned, in which each country brings its 'products'. I mean, this is something that might even look a bit ridiculous. When I first came to the biennale, I remember saying, 'What? How can such a thing work?' It's really something amusing. I had started to restore the Arsenale with the idea of having one large international exhibition, with different qualities to the spaces, so that it could be a great exhibition in which all countries could participate. But then this national phenomenon resurfaced, and now we are 77 countries this year. At least eight of them will be ready to build pavilions, but as there is no possibility of doing that in the Giardini I am offering an option to restore buildings in the Arsenale, so as to give permanent pavilions to a certain number of countries.

WM: And how is the Italian pavilion changing?

PB: I moved the Italian pavilion from the Giardini to the Arsenale, thus doubling its size, and that is the new Italian pavilion. The name 'Padiglione Italia' was confusing: if you translate it into English it becomes the Italian pavilion, though it's part of the international exhibition, and you don't have a chance to communicate this subtlety to the public. The name change also presented a way to solve a 'political problem'. The ministry wanted to step in more strongly and have its own pavilion. We said, so, let's be clear: this belongs to the international exhibition and this to the Italian pavilion.

AL: Can you talk about some of the other problems that you face in directing and overseeing the organisation of the biennale as an institution?

PB: Yes we face a certain number of problems, which have to do with the geopolitical evolution of the world and the different structures of government in each country. The US doesn't have a minister of culture, for instance, while Italy has at least three ministers of culture. The different constitutional models also affect the exhibition: the British pavilion is run by the British Council, while the US pavilion is run by their State Department and the Guggenheim Museum. We also have a problem with India, because they have Ministers of Culture for each of the different states, but culture is not a component of the central government. So right now we have letters coming in from India, but only from the local ministers. Then we have collateral exhibitions which are organised by foundations representing ethnic communities, which is to say, nations who don't recognise themselves in the state. And we also, of course, have exhibitions representing Palestine, Israel, Iran and so on, all side by side.

AL: Native Americans too…

PB: Yes, and we also have the Basques, the Iraqis, the Kurds and also the Formosans.

AL: Can you say 'no' to these requests for representation, or would that run counter to what you want the biennale to aspire to be?

PB: We say to them: 'We are glad you are here, because we really think that your presence is productive. But it's up to you not to provoke a political battle with the other countries and the Italian state.' But sometimes they do something that is provocative. I had to receive three ambassadors last year, saying to me, 'Now, why did you do that…'

AL: Writing about Gregotti's Molino Stucky exhibition of 1975, the president at the time, Carlo Ripa di Meana, wrote that one of the remarkable aspects of the biennale is that it has a self-reflexive capacity, and the biennale as an institution, much like its public, can learn from the exhibitions and the participating artists and architects as well. Of course it made sense for him to say something like this after 1968, when this self-reflexivity and responsiveness to the public would be demanded. But would you agree? Do you feel that the exhibitions teach you something about the institution as well?

PB: Each of them is really quite special in itself. I mean, I have seen curators who have covered the Arsenale with white walls, others who have been taking the walls off. Some have been thinking about the space and the work, and others haven't cared at all. And then there are those who were just ordering things as if it were a museum.

WM: Do you think that the biennale should reflect contemporary culture? Or should it lead culture and predict, in a way, what will be occupying the perspective of the vanguard?

PB: I have done both. After Fuksas's exhibition I asked Deyan Sudjic to curate, and his biennale reflected the current thinking on architecture at the time: we had discussed whether a biennale should always concentrate on what is going to happen in the future. But you cannot have the same thing every two years, and that is why I have turned to Sejima for the 2010 biennale. With Betsky's biennale, he took the critic's criticism of architecture to the extreme by arguing that today architecture is almost everything. The world is not one of building but of space and of things to be seen and heard and enjoyed. By contrast, in selecting Sejima, I chose an architect who is in fact one of the most architectural. She starts from the problem of architecture, and the question of how to define limits from inside and outside, or from two different outsides, or from two different insides. The freedom of architecture in dealing with space, in dividing space, is most elemental and strong. So Sejima seems to me to be an interesting choice, because with her we are returning to an architect who speaks about architecture and to some extent puts back on the table the basic questions which are not necessarily the most obvious recent questions about architecture. We are living in a moment when we are all talking about the city, urban development, technology, water rights, sprawl and so on. And you can organise in a fairly easy way exhibitions underlining these possible themes. But is this really the right way to organise an exhibition of architecture? No! Perhaps next year we will organise an exhibition of architecture that can be more active in the surroundings, that can get people more involved.

WM: What else are you planning for the 2010 architecture biennale?

PB: I plan to introduce discussions, meetings; and each Saturday will be dedicated to a former director of the biennale. The only one missing is of course Aldo Rossi. It is my way of asking, can you contribute to the question 'what is an exhibition of architecture?' It's not that one has to give a specific answer – it's a question to which there are always many possible solutions. The first ones didn't know whether the biennale should be an exhibition of specific projects and ideas or something larger. I am asking each of the previous directors to come back, and to rethink and start talking again about what each of them did and how their exhibitions were different.

WM: Francesco Dal Co said he had two years to prepare for his 1991 biennale, and explained how important it was to have that time. Today, there is so much less time available to each director.

PB: That is not in fact the problem. We are developing technology that is changing the time needed to create an exhibition. Sejima has a model of the Corderie in a room in her office in Japan, and she can see how it works if you put this or that in it. So the technology today helps – roughly 70 per cent of the work can be done by computer at this point. That being said, a biennale is a place where you meet things, where you touch things. If you lose that idea you don't need an exhibition. A biennale has to become, like Santiago de Compostela, a place of pilgrimage, a 'Mecca' where you have to go once in your life because the process of knowledge is completed by that sort of experience. You need to bring people together to talk and see each other. So this is my mission, to transform the biennale into a Santiago de Compostela. But this goes back to where we started: What are you coming to see? What should we offer you? Why are you coming to Santiago de Compostela? And once again this is the question of each biennale, and once again each biennale has its own answer. You know, I asked Harald Szeemann to curate two biennales in a row. I must say that even a genius like Szeemann had his problems in developing new and creative ideas for a second biennale. If you go beyond a certain number of years with the same curator, he begins to consider himself to be the only one who is capable of choosing and selecting what is new. And that is what we want to avoid. The formula of the biennale might seem a bit inefficient from some other point of view, but it is to keep a certain intensity, to keep changing the criteria.

AL: One of the most difficult things for us in organising the US pavilion was knowing that the public passes by so quickly. We hope that the exhibition will affect their senses and their mind, but we have such a short period of time to play with. Are you concerned with this? Does it seem specific to the technological moment in which we live?

PB: In logic, a problem which is an inevitable problem disappears as a problem.

AL: You mean that it is simply the reality today?

PB: Once again we are back to the question of what a visit to the biennale is. I cannot pretend that if you start in the morning and end in the evening you will see everything with complete attention, fully entering into a spirit of understanding what is there. Therefore the role of the theatrical capability of the curator is fundamental, because it is this capability which makes for a good or bad exhibition. When you think back upon what you saw, it's not that you need to fully digest it all, because that would be like reading a book. The biennale is simply too large. We have to live today with an unsolvable problem, which sometimes might appear as a setback. We simply do not have enough time today to fully appreciate what is going on. A curator should not make compromises, and should live with these contradictions, because these contradictions make us very modern. We must live with the problems to which we have no solutions. This is as true in politics as it is in economics and the modern world. I am not afraid of living with this, but I am afraid of those who want to solve everything, and who do not leave any possibilities to the visitor. You think that curating is like writing an essay, and that people should come in and start at the beginning and progress through to the conclusion? This is not an exhibition model that can help you, not here. We have to be quite clear, I am really interested in problems with no obvious solutions. I leave total freedom to the curator, but I always am clear about the problems that they have to face. I encourage them to involve their imagination, and not only rationality. If you want to develop workshops or seminars to think about these things, that's okay. But the visual part of the exhibition is more effective in speaking to the public in an emotional way. Have you seen this biennale by Birnbaum, and what he is doing there in the Corderie? He is one of the most interesting curators I have ever seen. With the Corderie, you can easily fall into the trap of anxiety about empty spaces – I've had exhibitions where the curators were obsessed with putting different things on white walls. Birnbaum, on the other hand, understands the complexity of what it means to do a biennale; he understands that there is such a rich history, and that this means that you need to justify the current articulation. He understands the complexity of the problematic – that, in a certain sense, the biennale is exhausted because there have been so many iterations. The challenge is to reinvigorate it each year, and sometimes to be sufficiently naïve. In particular you find there that the whole Corderie is a traditional *passegiata*. A *passegiata* through fancy, through fantasy, through fairy tales.

AL: He was one of the very first curators to also accept that we don't know what a work of art is anymore, because today it can be absolutely anything.

PB: I think he was so good because he really showed us that artists are a bit lost in creativity: they have left behind the idea of being the saviours of the world, the interpreters of the tragedies of contemporary life. Birnbaum has been perfect in that reading, and in therefore having no anxiety about the empty space. He has been using the Corderie like the third act of Mozart's *Magic Flute*, where you have this walking experience of emotions. He has really lived with the instruments we have given him in the most clever way.

WM: Did he work closely with each of the artists to make this theatrical experience what it was?

PB: Yes, he discussed with each artist the size and the dimensions of each piece. To be a curator really means to be a director of a theatre, and to make a sort of artwork. You have to discuss everything with everyone: how much, where, this or that? I liked this Corderie because it gives the exact sensation of present time, and the sense of artists who have become lost in creativity with no more guidelines. These artists were retreating to some sort of incredible individualism. Artists were painting themselves, their wives, their friends, their mothers, their homes, where they live. They turned their eyes toward themselves, as if we were once again in *Alice in Wonderland*. These artists were lost in a world of objects and colours, and the title of the show, 'Making Worlds', was a perfect representation of that because each was making his own world. But all this is not obvious when you begin, because there is no recipe. It's not something that you can codify, and you cannot say, 'This is the formula. Please, next curator, apply it.'

AL: Would you ever consider selecting more than one curator for the biennale?

PB: No, I cannot work with a team of curators, because then all the tension is lost. I am for one man, one show, and one responsibility. If you give them this chance and freedom, curators feel as if they are artists with their own work of art to be imagined. Therefore, co-curatorship is a wrong form, and I will never adopt it. Even with that size of task, one man is a prerequisite for this responsibility, which is at once moral, aesthetic and administrative. Now we don't have the money to pay all the costs of what we show. Last year we rewrote the regulations on funding for the exhibitions: we divide the cost of the curator, the cost of the exhibition from the point of view of the curator, and all the rest. Then we have a certain sum for, let's say, each installation; make an average, and that is the cost. Of course, the money is not sufficient. The Gehry installation last year was built by our people, and the cost of that was almost eight times what was allotted. This meant that he had to help organise some of the funding. But you cannot fill the Corderie, you cannot fill the theatre, if you do not spend money. So the curator has to use their ability in imagining whom to bring there and what to invite him to do, while at the same finding money to do what he wants to do. For this reason, we have developed over the last two years in particular relations with an incredible number of foundations that help artists, and it is the responsibility of the curator to engage with them. We call the potential artists who come to the biennale the roots, trunk and sprouts. For the roots, we have to give money because we have to take them out of museums. For sprouts, we give money. The trunks, well they have to pay, because they are already in a position where they can find money, and for them being at the biennale really means something to their collectors. For the young ones, we pay, and we even give a sum that is larger than what we pay the famous artists. And we always have a certain number of young artists, managed according to criteria which are very simple.

Afterword

William Menking

The ten Venice Biennale curators interviewed
for this project seem to agree on only one thing
– the impossibility of creating exhibitions on
architecture. Confronted with tremendous
responsibilities, chronic underfunding and a
breakneck schedule, why did they take it on?
The temptation to put on a show is probably real
enough. Aaron Betsky suggests that 'when the
huge wooden doors of the empty Arsenale are
opened and you are presented with a half a mile
of medieval, high-vaulted, brick-columned space,
you can't turn down the opportunity to fill that
space'. Then there's the city of Venice itself, with
its legendary architectural associations and the
heritage of the 100-year-old biennale. But these
are not the only factors attracting these figures
– all with distinguished reputations of their own –
to try and prove themselves here on a scale larger
than most had ever encountered before. It is more
likely that they agreed, or sought, to participate
because the Venice Biennale is the one event where
the entire architecture world – practitioners, critics,
academics, students and others – comes together
to present, look at and debate architecture. Simply
put, it is the most established and prestigious
event in the world of architecture and curating,

and represents a crowning achievement for any career.

But despite its current pre-eminence in architectural culture, the origins of the biennale, as Aaron Levy points out, are rooted in radical politics. In 1968 politically engaged students beseiged the gates of the art biennale, protesting that the exhibition had become elitist and detached from reality. As the organisers believed that architecture had more potential to connect with day-to-day problems and conditions, they asked Vittorio Gregotti to curate – create, actually – an architecture-inspired event. The 1976 Molino Stucky competition was the result. But even Gregotti, curator of the critically important 1964 Milan Triennale, argues in his interview that when it comes to presenting architecture, 'Communication with the public is practically impossible.' And at the time – and given his politics – it still seems a strange choice to ask Gregotti to lead the way in making these connections.

Gregotti's dilemma turned out to be a recurring one. Every biennale curator that we interviewed described the difficulty of presenting this 'specialised field' to a broader public but then proceeded to do just that: create a poplar exhibition for a public of non-specialists. All argued that their own biennales were popular in a 'new way'. Most of these were only semantic differences (presenting the historical versus the modern), but they also projected real and strongly felt positions regarding the conditions of architecture current at the time and the problem of how to make these clear to audiences including both architects and non-designers.

Paolo Portoghesi, for example, told us that it was modern architecture that had 'lost the possibility to speak to the common people'. He went on to say that giving people 'only a statistical idea about the role of the citizen in the world is not useful, it's not indicative of the beauty of the biennale, which is about artistic culture'. This might be read as a critique of exhibitions that catalogued current urban projects (Sudjic) or foregrounded statistics (Burdett), but more to the point Portoghesi was arguing that with architecture there is always the possibility of direct communication between people and architects, between people and architecture. 'Architecture for architects', he argued, 'is wrong, and it breaks the continuity of architectural history. Architecture is not for architects; it's for the public.' His 1980 *Strada Novissima* was his attempt to present a different way of connecting modern architecture with history and the public.

All the curators in fact believed that they were connecting to the public. And so it comes down to how they made it happen. Hans Hollein, for example, said, 'My biennale was the first one that had a new audience.' He presumably meant that his was not just for professional designers but was an attempt to showcase avant-garde work of his day. Both Burdett and Sudjic argued that their presentations were aimed at bringing the conditions and experiences of architecture to the general public. Even Aaron Betsky and perhaps Kazuyo Sejima focused on the work created by the perceived avant-garde while framing it for public education and consumption.

The biennale exhibitions that work best, president of the biennale Paolo Baratta argues, are the ones that are the most cinematic and entertaining. While this may be a desirable goal for a public exhibition, it is equally true that the best exhibits are the ones that inspire without preaching. This leaves us with a Venice Biennale that tumbles together not only the most radical, experimental and design-focused propositions, but also the kind of work most likely to speak to the public about everyday experiences. How well the biennale achieves this every other year is the reason for going to Venice yourself.

Colophon

Architecture on Display: On The History of
The Venice Biennale of Architecture

Managing Editor: Thomas Weaver
Publications Editor: Pamela Johnston
Art Director: Zak Kyes
Design: Wayne Daly
Editorial Assistant: Clare Barrett

Titles set in Maria, designed by Phil Baber
Text set in Elzivir
Printed in Denmark by Norhaven A/S

ISBN 978-1-902902-96-8

For a catalogue of AA Publications visit
www.aaschool.ac.uk/publications
or email publications@aaschool.ac.uk

AA Publications, 36 Bedford Square
London WC1B 3ES
T + 44 (0)20 7887 4021
F + 44 (0)20 7414 0783

SLOUGHT
FOUNDATION